A
PONY
IN THE
BEDROOM

of related interest

Pretending to be Normal (Second Edition)
Living with Asperger's Syndrome (Autism Spectrum Disorder)
Liane Holliday Willey
Foreword by Tony Attwood
ISBN 978 1 84905 755 4
eISBN 978 0 85700 987 6

Safety Skills for Asperger Women
How to Save a Perfectly Good Female Life
Liane Holliday Willey
Foreword by Tony Attwood
ISBN 978 1 84905 836 0
eISBN 978 0 85700 327 0

Nerdy, Shy, and Socially Inappropriate
A User Guide to an Asperger Life
Cynthia Kim
ISBN 978 1 84905 757 8
eISBN 978 0 85700 949 4

Short Stories about Alcohol, Asperger Syndrome, and God
Tessie Regan
ISBN 978 1 84905 761 5
eISBN 978 0 85700 951 7

A
PONY
IN THE
BEDROOM

A JOURNEY THROUGH ASPERGER'S, ASSAULT, AND HEALING WITH HORSES

SUSAN DUNNE

FOREWORD BY
LIANE HOLLIDAY WILLEY

Jessica Kingsley *Publishers*
London and Philadelphia

First published in 2015
by Jessica Kingsley Publishers
73 Collier Street
London N1 9BE, UK
and
400 Market Street, Suite 400
Philadelphia, PA 19106, USA

www.jkp.com

Library of Congress Cataloging in Publication Data
Dunne, Susan.
  A pony in the bedroom : a journey through Asperger's, assault, and healing with horses
/ Susan Dunne.
     pages cm
  ISBN 978-1-84905-609-0 (alk. paper)
  1. Dunne, Susan--Mental health. 2. Asperger's syndrome--Patients--Biography. 3. Post-
traumatic stress
disorder--Patients--Biography. 4. Victims of violent crime--Biography. 5. Rape victims--
Biography. 6.
Horses--Therapeutic use. I. Title.
  RC553.A88D85 2015
  616.85'88320092--dc23
  [B]
                            2014036671

British Library Cataloguing in Publication Data
A CIP catalogue record for this book is available from the British Library

ISBN 978 1 84905 609 0
eISBN 978 1 78450 076 4

Printed and bound in the United States

contents

foreword

Hippotherapy, or equine therapy, relies on a horse as the therapist. Riding, grooming, caring for and just simply bonding with a massively strong and yet sensitive four-legged friend has been quantitatively proven to assist a human through a wide range of physical and emotional therapies and rehabilitations. Though there are myriad hippotherapy programmes with many different facets and approaches, they are all based on the simple principle that a horse's large and small movements, along with the warmth from his body, provide the human with sensory information that wakes and encourages positive neurophysiological systems. When riding, one's core strength, balance, hand–eye coordination, fine motor skills, body awareness, ability to concentrate, interpersonal communication and general language skills, self-esteem, executive functioning skills, patience, self-control and sensory integration improve, while anxiety and depression decrease. But riding isn't the only way to reach valuable enrichment. Indeed, simply handling or physically interacting with an equine can cue heaps of positive emotional benefits. Together, horses and people make a magical mixture of supports naturally tailored for people with autism spectrum disorders.

That's the quantifiable side of horses healing people, but for anyone who has had a horse for a friend, the healing properties are immeasurable. Much like myself, Susan Dunne found her first horse friend when she was only a toddler. Susan's first ride was on top of a white pony on a beach. Mine was with Prince, a black and white paint pony. Those faithful equines showed two little humans how life was meant to feel. They gave us our first feeling of reverent awe. They gave us the spark of what it means to be connected to another living creature.

Childhood games, rhyming bedtime stories, toys in shiny wrappers, sparkly holiday parties, the thrill of making new schoolmates – all of those early-life events drift into oblivion when compared to the sheer joy that comes from being a horse's friend. There is no cure for a girl obsessed with horses. Time between visits with our kindred spirit may pass into years, but memories and thoughts of who they are and what they mean to us will stand still. Once a horse has imprinted on a human, there is no denying or forgetting the connection.

Much like Susan, I had given up my need for an actual horse after my children were born. For 18 years I only met with the occasional carriage horse or policeman's steed for a gentle nuzzle and a luscious consumption of all things horse. The leather tack. The packed hooves that inevitably smell of dirt and manure. The big horse teeth stained with the colour and scent of green hay. Spying a swatch of sweat just beneath the point where the saddle pad meets the horse's back. A mane, thick or thin, long or short, braided or not, but always something to play with. Soulful eyes that can probably read your thoughts. And the sounds, like the clicking of the hooves against pavement or pasture, or the snort and the whinny just before the horse trills his lips. For 18 years I let all those things, so rich and real, fill me up with just enough horse love to float me through some hard times. Susan did this, too. She let her special interest in horses give her mind a much-needed respite even if she wasn't enjoying a hands-on horse experience. What a cool lesson for everyone: a special interest can still make us happy even if it can only be a memory.

Sadly, but typically for those of us on the spectrum, Susan had many hard times. With graceful intent and vivid detail, she shares her difficult times with her readers, steeping us in their rough waters. Her stories resonate with me just as I'm sure they will resonate with others who have an autism spectrum diagnosis. I couldn't help but think *me too* as I moved through her book. Sometimes it was as if I was looking at my own past. Susan reminds us that though surely each person is unique, we share commonalities that connect us all. That's nice. It's comforting.

While moving through the tough parts keep this in mind: Susan's story of horses that heal will follow, and when it does, you will be cheered. In fact, you might even learn a new thing or two about animal therapy; things you may wish to include in your life or in the lives of people you care for, no matter their need or diagnosis.

This is a book that reaches beyond autism. It's a book for anyone and everyone who loves animals, happy endings and the human spirit.

Liane Holliday Willey,
author of *Pretending to be Normal*

acknowledgments

Like most people on the autism spectrum, my contact with people can vary from the sketchy to the non-existent, as the following story will show, but I'm particularly grateful to the following:

To those who've shared in my love of horses, especially Gwen, Joyce, Ellie and Rose from the St Ives Riding for the Disabled in Bingley, who provided such brilliant human- and horse-handling skills when taking the ponies into the strangest places; special thanks to Joy Birch, who did the above and beyond, and makes a brilliant cappuccino at the St Ives Café near Bingley, and to Joe, Judith and Angie, the Wild West Yorkshire Cowboys.

Extra special thanks to fellow horse addict Karen Garrad for so many *mitzvahs* and for turning the *folie à une* of autism into occasional bouts of *folie à deux* – they were fun. Also for some much-needed Jewish humour in darker moments – oy.

To Rosy and Karen, for just being great people.

To Dr Jeremy Hyde, consultant psychiatrist at the Airedale Mental Health District, who diagnosed me with Asperger's and had the sense and sensitivity not to prescribe me a course of normality to be taken three times a day. Knowing the cause has made all the difference.

To James, for sharing the winter wilderness years ago and for those amazing conversations about life, literature and why we were so socially incompetent.

To Lee and Gav, the farrier boys, for a monthly dose of lads' talk – it's been educational and nearly worth what you charge me in horseshoes.

To everyone at Autism First in West Yorkshire, for the brilliant work you do.

And most of all:

To Bailey, Misty, Alfie, Spot and Coco, the horses who enter my silent space every day, remain silent and always leave it enhanced. If you knew how special you were, you wouldn't be so special (though, Coco, I would prefer it if you'd walk round me instead of through me once in a while).

To the memory of Minder, Ollie, Henry, Poppy and especially Dessie, my dog of a lifetime. If there's a heaven, you'd better all be there or I'm not coming.

For most of my life I've lived in two alternative worlds – an inner, private and closed-off one and the outer social world. Being on the autism spectrum, and born at a time when the term Asperger's was recognised only in remote medical circles, I've had to learn to live in both worlds. As I'm on the milder end of the spectrum, where superficially at least I can pass off as your average if slightly odd person for some of the time (it's true: no one fools everyone all of the time), I've spent a lifetime trying to work out how to function in both worlds. I've got by, stumbled through without a map or a guidebook and fallen into quite a few potholes and snake pits along the way.

I am not a natural hermit or recluse, but because being around others is often an exhausting and overwhelming experience I prefer to spend the majority of my time alone. Navigating through the intricacies of social niceties, the rules of small talk, the subtler aspects of facial expressions and body language has never come naturally. For most of my life I have failed to see the point of it all, regarding interaction with others as something only to be done for a specific purpose, keeping it as short and functional as possible. Social situations have often been frustrating, sometimes seeming pointless, irritating and boring, and sometimes terrifying ordeals to be endured, feeling that I had none of the necessary social knowhow to help get me through. Put simply, being alone feels safe, manageable and comfortable, and being with others is often risky, overwhelming and uncomfortable.

But, of course, it isn't that simple. No woman is an island – well, not completely. As a human, even one on the autistic spectrum, you are part of an essentially social species. The struggle (and it is a lifelong one) lies in trying to strike the delicate balance between being overwhelmed and engulfed by human contact and suffering the debilitating effects of extreme isolation. It is a fine tightrope walk between the two, and most of my life has been spent falling to one side or other of the fine line that separates the two worlds.

My solution has always been to try to keep the two worlds separate, alternately existing in one and then the other, whilst at all costs trying to avoid letting the two collide and thus create what I feared would be a personal catastrophic explosion. I don't know exactly why I felt I had to spend my life undertaking the more-than-human task of holding two worlds separate – even Atlas only had to keep one going at a time – but I believe the need to keep these worlds separate stemmed from fear bordering on terror. The barriers of the inner autistic world keep me safe: too much from the outside leads to an implosion, a shattering of the self into infinite fine shards which can only be painstakingly put back together by retreat and a prolonged withdrawal. This is the story of how one world (the external) overran the other (my private inner world) and how I was forced to renegotiate my path between the two.

Some years ago I was the victim of a life-threatening attack which led to severe post-traumatic stress. The assault left me unable to retreat into the safe autistic world that I had created, but nor could I reach out to the external world from which I seemed to be forever excluded. It was a seemingly hopeless situation in which I felt I was doomed to an existence in some strange, peripheral no-man's-land, a ghost caught between earthly existence and eternity. At this time a chance question from a doctor, simple in itself but life-changing in its consequences, sent me in search of my unfulfilled childhood obsession: horses. What follows is an account of how, through horses, I moved out of a frozen, traumatised space and went on to find a place between the two worlds, a liminal space where, paradoxically, I could feel at home, where I was neither stuck in my own isolated world, which sometimes felt empty and incomplete, nor overwhelmed in a social world not of my own choosing. Horses allowed me to enter the herd without demands or expectations and to see the herd as a place of safety and inclusion. Horses have not cured my autism – there is no cure: it is a pervasive developmental disorder which affects you for life – and I still have to exist for the most part in two separate worlds, but horses have offered me a Between Space, a place to go to each and every day that has brought me peace and sanctuary and, most importantly in the autistic world, a sense of connectedness.

To understand this, first a few words about the two worlds. By far my preferred world is the inner private one and the comfort and safety of isolation. In the safe sphere of my own skull I have a self to call my own. There I can be alone, uninterrupted and free to explore the limitless inner territory. Shutting the door on the outside world and retreating to my inner one is always done with immense relief, any interruption viewed with fear, loathing or annoyance. My inner world is mainly silent. I dislike unnecessary noise, such as a background TV channel or people talking, because it distracts me from the intense internal focus. Even a noise outside on the street can disturb me.

But what do you do when you're in there, shut into this private Party for One? In the absence of social interests, you have to fill your time somehow. Being at the higher-functioning/Asperger end of the autistic spectrum, I'm quite adept at providing my own entertainment in the form of whatever obsessive interest possesses me at the time – in popular belief this is your average trainspotter, but I am not mono-focussed, tending more towards serial interests. Some have been distinctly niche (Bactrian camels and learning Yiddish come to mind), some broad-sweeping, covering wide periods of history and literature, others distinctly on the odd side. I've learned eight languages for fun (which is ironic as I don't speak without good cause), learned reams of dates and facts off by heart, and could currently tell you (should you care to listen) exactly how many spots my Dalmatian, Dessie, had. Sad, I know, but no matter – an obsession is an obsession so you might as well just give in to it and learn all about it. A few have spanned a lifetime, including English literature and horses (more, much more on horses later), and others have been fleeting (the mating ritual of tortoises is a concise subject), but, whatever the current focus is, I will for a time be completely mono-focussed – no interruptions welcome, *Do Not Disturb* sign hung up on the forehead.

People are rarely if ever invited to share this inner world: it is a strictly *By Invitation Only* party, all family and friends excluded from the guest list. Quite simply, I don't feel the need to share it, or maybe I fear it would be ruined if I did, believing that if someone else was allowed in, I would be ousted or disempowered. I am rarely bored or lonely in it. Retreating back into my inner world always feels like a homecoming, Ithaca after an external odyssey. It is the chance to let go and breathe deeply again, to shake off the outside world in what feels almost like a purifying process – a kind of decontaminating isolation, a quarantine for the soul.

The following story may seem scant on people, the normal people who populate normal lives: family, friends, work colleagues, neighbours, the casual day-to-day encounters that happen in an average day for most people – or, to paraphrase Holden Caulfield in *The Catcher in the Rye*, all that *David Copperfield* stuff. The reason for this absence is partly that in my unsocial world I have far fewer contacts than most people appear to have – I have spent vast tracts of my life alone. But the lack of human population in this book is also because, on a subjective level, I habitually screen people out when they are not with me (and, if need be, when they are). This isn't a conscious mechanism; perhaps it is just a basic self- (for that, read autistic) preservation mechanism. Too much contact and I feel overloaded, and in my autistic world a very little can go a very long way. A quirk in my mental processing means that for the most part I retain only an objective memory of most people I come into contact with when I am not with them, so that when I retreat into myself I lack any subjective experience of others: they remain abstractions, peripheral at least, non-existent at most. It's as if a pair of sliding doors automatically shut themselves between me and others when I need to retreat.

So much for the inner world.

But whilst the sirens of the inner world are always calling me, I am not free from that other outer world – that 'blooming, buzzing confusion', as William James characterised it, with all its noise, mess and rush. In the outer world I grew up feeling that I became other people's property, powerless and vulnerable and deprived of self-determination. One persistent nightmare that has recurred frequently throughout my life captures this sense well. In the dream I am a prisoner waiting in line with many others. The guards are looking for someone to shoot. They may choose me. In the dream I am frozen in terror, desperately willing myself to be invisible, not to think or to blink or to breathe in case they look at me, make eye contact, single me out. The shutting down in the dream is an extreme version of what seems to happen so often in waking moments, when fear and a sense of powerlessness lead me to implode, turn inwards in fear. Too much human eye contact and I could, Medusa-style, turn to stone. Sometimes the only defence is to go on the offensive by becoming rude, aggressive, domineering. It works, but only up to a point.

One of the main reasons living in the outer world has been much more problematic is that people with autism are often hypersensitive to it. This world grates and jars on the senses – it's easy to feel overwhelmed by a voice that is too loud, someone standing too close, too much eye contact for too long, unsought physical contact, conversations that go on too long, someone breathing… In fact, any and every outside sensory stimulus is a potential red flag. Nature, however, has provided me with one main advantage: being small, I usually fall below the line of direct eye contact for most people. I've always considered this a great bonus in a world where looks could kill.

In other areas I'm not always so lucky. Because I'm caught between the two worlds rather than able to wholly opt for one or the other, and am still dependent on this outer world to feed me and pay the rent, I have at least to try to tolerate being in social and work situations some of the time. It isn't easy. Conversations that go on too long, meetings that never seem to end, having to share the office canteen, the lift, the same space – the same oxygen, damn it! – for a set number of hours can be draining and overloading. Sometimes the only option is to shut down. Shutdown begins in silence, an obstinate selective mutism, a failure to engage in facial contact, and if the source does not go away and I can't escape, I cease to listen, cease to feel. Better still, I bunk off early, jack in the job, ring in sick. Being on the autistic spectrum has sabotaged my career prospects something rotten.

And then there are social situations… The freewheeling absence of clear guidelines as to what exactly do you say after you've said hello always leaves me with a sense of rising panic. When it comes to being with people in any capacity other than one with a fixed and specific purpose, I often fail to grasp the give-and-take currency of social interactions, usually feeling bankrupt and waiting for the debt collectors to come in. I have often remained oblivious to the unwritten social rules which say honesty is only acceptable up to a point, being with others can be an end in itself, parties are not about retreating into a corner with a glass of wine and a book.

Over time and with increased exposure, I have learned the language of social communication in the human sphere, much as you would learn a foreign language. I have become passably fluent, and as I have become more proficient, I can often pass off as a native speaker. But I still lack the subtle nuances of the true native: the turns of phrase, the unusual idioms, the metaphors of social discourse that mark out the truly bilingual from the merely fluent. I have never become a native of this world but these days, after a lifetime of practice, I can do a tolerable pastiche. Still, constantly speaking in a foreign language is hard work and at any given social gathering I'm most likely to commune with a passing cat or dog, or, failing that, head off for the bookcase again.

In contrast to humans, I have always been strangely drawn towards animals, willing to get physically close, communicate with them and – something which so rarely happens with humans – just enjoy being in their presence without fear or anxiety or a need to plan an escape route. Compared with humans, the demands and expectations of animals are manageable, straightforward and meetable, and don't leave me feeling torn, compromised or wanting in some way; animals in turn can meet my needs for contact and communication. I don't take a sentimental view of animals or regard them as in some way providing the same mental stimulus that comes from human interaction – discussing metaphysics with animals is not an option, but then I don't feel much need to discuss metaphysics with people either, books being my preferred option. But nor do I regard animals as in some way inferior to humans: they are themselves in a way that few humans can ever attain to be. The unconditional acceptance that animals can bring, free of the unspoken, unwritten but ever-present social demands is peace indeed in a lifetime of draining struggle to operate in a world whose rationale frequently evades me.

Getting to the point where I could share my world with horses (or, more accurately, they had the grace to share theirs with mine) and thereby transform it has been a long and difficult journey. As an autistic person operating in a neurotypical world, I've encountered a large number of snares and traps, been hampered by social naivety and the absence of a human safety network. My early adult years as described in the first part of this book, when I was let loose in the world and somehow had to find my way in it alone, are testimony to this. That isn't to say, however, that along the way I wasn't often the recipient of many unsought kindnesses from both humans and animals, spontaneously given and demanding nothing in return. These moments of kindness have often thrown me a lifeline, usually in times of greatest need. On the surface they may seem small, soon forgotten or simply inconsequential, but they constantly served to remind me that, no matter how deep into the wilderness we may be, we are never wholly beyond reach and our worst moments can sometimes be the ones of greatest redemption and transformation.

To all those who tried to reach out to me in my closed-off world along the way, my sincerest thanks. It may have seemed a thankless task – none of it went unnoticed.

Part 1

All the World Before Me

I

social misfit

I was 18 and about to enter the adult world, but there was one major drawback – I felt about eight years old. I hadn't spoken to anyone in my peer group for three months since leaving school, lacked most of the essential social graces supposedly mastered by the age of ten and did not have a single friend.

It did not bode well.

The sliding doors of the train taking me away to university slid shut and, as they did, so did those in my mind creating a see-through barrier on the past. I carried no one inside me – I was too afraid. It made me seem cold, aloof, cut off; it turned me into a black sheep excluding and excluded from the family fold, an outsider to the pen. But it kept me safe. As the world I had known all my life – that of people and family and places – receded through the train windows, it also receded from my mind in a strange blocking-out process. It was a process I knew well.

I turned my gaze away from the past and focussed on the future: the place I was going to be living in from now on. In my rucksack I had brought with me a private currency of ten favourite books, one change of clothes (as an afterthought) and a packet of Marlboro cigarettes. In my mind I brought a vague dream of a future not spent entirely alone, a place of safety and connectedness, a sense of belonging in the incomprehensible world I lived in.

The optimism I had in those days never ceases to amaze me.

Smash! It was hard work driving a stake through her body, but after four or five attempts I succeeded. The attack was nothing personal – I just wanted to see if the doll bled like everyone else. I was six at the time; lots of things like that intrigued me when I was six.

The impaled naked doll splayed out on the railings wasn't bleeding, so that solved that one, then. My curiosity satisfied, I turned my attention to the movement of a pink worm emerging from the earth and abandoned the doll to her fate. I wasn't drawn to a poor, plastic imitation of a person any more than I was drawn to the flesh-and-blood types that milled around outside the private bubble I lived in.

At that age I had a small brown bear called Bruin and with him it was different. He was a stern-looking bear, hard and inflexible, but he had one great advantage over any doll: he had fur – coarse, short, dark brown fur, so much better than white imitation or human flesh. The other thing I liked was Lego: the creative opportunities it presented struck me as far more interesting than the supposed maternal arts that go with having dolls, and I spent a lot of time trying to construct horses in red and white bricks. Unfortunately, Lego is too angular and horses too curvaceous for it to work to any satisfactory degree, so I compromised and built horse carriages instead – the wheels, like those of the Flintstones, were on the square side, but no matter, I liked things with wheels. Already at six I had an impressive collection of Dinky cars which I would line up against the skirting board in a never-changing order. There was security in order – at least, order of your own creation.

It was starting to rain, the dreary drizzle that only a Lancashire grey sky can produce. The next-door neighbour, an elderly spinster who was headmistress of a primary school, came out to take in her washing. Seeing the impaled doll, she came over. I felt myself go rigid, the beginning of a minor implosion that would occur throughout my life at unsought human encounters. Already I was focussing on a scratch on the black paint of the wooden fence, looking at it so intently that the voice came as if from nowhere – distant, disembodied.

'Does she have a name?'

'Zebra.' I stared at the scratch.

'Do you mean Deborah?'

I probably did. Someone somewhere must have named the stupid thing. I would have preferred a zebra anyway. Like Bruin, zebras had hair, not flesh, and they had one other supreme attribute – four legs.

The elderly lady looked up at the sky. The rain was coming down more heavily.

'It's raining cats and dogs!' she said jovially.

I looked up at the sky, hoping that a Dalmatian would land on the lawn (Walt Disney had recently introduced me to 101 of them). It didn't. Why did people get your hopes up like that? It was just one more reason for preferring animals. The rain came down and the impaled doll stayed outside, getting wet.

There were no zebras roaming the streets of urban Lancashire where I grew up in the 1960s and '70s: the nearest most people got to an equine was a donkey ride on the beach at Blackpool once a year. An early photo album shows me as a two-year-old, sitting on a white pony at Morecambe beach. My feet don't reach the stirrups. Judging by the expression on my face, I have reached a kind of two-year-old heaven – a private heaven. I am not looking up at the world around me.

I grew up in a largely animal-free zone (give or take a couple of older siblings who, being bipeds, didn't really count). Over the years a number of beasts swam, crept and crawled in – mostly goldfish, tadpoles and a garden hedgehog – the freebie wildlife pets of the petless kid. At one point a tortoise was acquired. Hifi, for so he was called, was a compromise pet who lived in a box in the shed and required little in the way of maintenance, care or talking to. For a child on the autistic spectrum (even though this wasn't realised at the time), a tortoise was an inspired choice: cold-blooded, self-contained, equipped with a ready-made shelter-for-one and prone to hibernate for long stretches.

It wasn't, though, as I recall, a particularly satisfactory situation. This eclectic childhood taxonomy was all well and good, but what I really wanted was something with fur and four legs, preferably something that lived in a stable. Once, after one of the many fights I got into with my older sister (fights I was always destined to lose, being smaller), my mother drew attention to the fact that we were lucky to have one another, pointing out that my father, who had been an only child, had not been so lucky.

'He had a dog,' I said, recalling tales of him adopting a stray Dalmatian.

'That's not the same,' my mother said. 'A sister is a lot more important than a dog.' I wasn't convinced. Some years later, reading Orwell's *Animal Farm*, it struck me that the sheep-bleating slogan 'Four legs good, two legs bad' was fairly self-evident.

The horse I longed for never came. No amount of placing it at the top of my Christmas or birthday list was going to produce one. I tried adding it to the weekly shopping list for a while, so that along with tea bags and fish fingers there would be 'Horse for Susan' added on, but my pester power failed to yield any results. In the absence of the real thing, I dreamed instead that a white pony would just turn up in my bedroom one day, standing by my bed, joining all the other plastic and ceramic and paper herds which filled the drawers, the shelves, the wardrobe, the walls. The dream pony was big and powerful, invariably white, with a flowing mane and tail. He snorted fire from his magnificent nostrils, pawed the ground with his immense hoof, impatient to take me on a journey through the clouds. Sometimes he had wings, sometimes he was a unicorn, but always he was mine, exclusively mine, and no one could take him away from me. In those days my imagination wasn't hung up on details like feed and hay nets and mucking out, and the reality was I would have happily settled for any broken-winded old carthorse with three legs, but none came my way. Now, when I take white ponies into people's bedrooms fairly regularly (more on this strange fact later), I often hear people recall the same childhood fantasy.

I remained obsessed with horses for some years. Eventually, I gave up for want of opportunity and the childhood dream was buried – many years later I would discover that it had been buried alive, that it was still a living, breathing passion just waiting to be exhumed. Horses were not in the interim replaced by a need to reach out to the human world. As I grew older, I increasingly turned inwards, living in a world of reading and thought. The few friends I had fell by the wayside as the inner world consumed me. I felt little connection to the world going on around me and felt detached from family and social connections which offered no competition for the riches of my inner world. But it came at a price. I became increasingly locked in on myself, unable to communicate, and as I withdrew more and more, I failed to acquire the necessary social skills that would equip me for the adult world I was about to enter.

As I sat on the train heading down south, I celebrated my rite of passage into the adult world by buying a whisky from the train buffet bar and lighting up my first cigarette in public. I breathed deeply; it felt good. Freedom and opportunity beckoned. The train rattled on, taking me, so I believed, towards *The Future* – the place where I believed it was all going to be better.

Disillusionment took a matter of weeks.

The social rules were confusing. After the initial meetings with people on my course in the English department and in the ivy-covered red-brick hall of residence where I lived, I wasn't quite sure what to do when I saw them again. Perhaps just smiling would have been as good a starting point as any, but I rarely if ever smiled. Partly this was from fear – I lived in a world of heightened anxiety – but it was also because, in my autistic reasoning, it was just another part of an incomprehensible social jigsaw. Smiling felt like a stupid submissive gesture that people used in the other world to ingratiate themselves, and I didn't want to ingratiate myself; I wanted to keep a safe distance around me. If people got too close, I risked being overwhelmed and engulfed – better to look a miserable cow than risk being annihilated. The most people would get off me would be a terrified fleeting rictus flashing across my face, devoid of eye contact, and an immediate looking away.

I had similar problems with talking. First, I didn't really understand the need to talk – if you weren't talking for a purely functional purpose, why were you wasting time with it? Second, I often struggled just to speak anyway: speech was something I had to dredge up from so deep down inside me that it rarely seemed worth the effort, and lack of practice did not make me a scintillating conversationalist. Once drawn to the surface, words lacked any of the meaning they had had inside me and, besides, by then the conversation had usually moved on to something else, so in general it was better to say nothing in the first place.

Silence did not help me make friends. I listened to others talking around me and concluded, like Hamlet, that it was just 'Words, words, words' – pointless, noisy and irritating but, for some reason that I could not fathom, regarded as worthy, meaningful and pleasant.

I had no grasp then of the social chit-chat that oils the wheels of communication and acts as a testing ground before more is said and revealed, and in those days I hadn't yet learned to fake interest where none existed. The only time I would spontaneously talk was in the exchange of ideas, the neutral territory of knowledge and thought which was what had always interested me more than any social interaction.

Now that I was sharing communal living quarters with a peer group for the first time, I was beginning to find out that there was a social expectation that you do things with others. I discovered that you were supposed to walk to the library and go for coffee together, you sat in each other's rooms talking, listening to music, and you ate meals together, and it was all as natural as breathing. The problem was it left me choking. In my self-propelling world you just did something – other people held you up or (worse) talked to you or wanted something called company seemingly for the sake of it.

Bemused, I watched the social process going on around me in those first few weeks. Initial encounters mutated into friendships, partnerships and social groups. In the early days, in that initial desperate rush that everyone was making to form friends, to be seen to be socially successful, I was invited along, but I rarely if ever got asked back. Much of the time when I was in groups was spent hiding away somewhere – usually the bathroom where the presence of mirrors allowed me to check that I was still myself in what I invariably found to be a fragmenting experience. So I remained peripheral to it all, still in the place where I had always been – alone. A change of scenery did not change me into a social being, as I had believed on some level it would, and that world I'd dreamed of inheriting dangled before me, palpable but beyond me, like a merry-go-round that never stopped. All the pretty prancing horses, the fun of the fair, the carousel music continued as I stood on the sidelines, watching it spinning round and round without me. Inside a voice was starting to howl in protest: *It was all supposed to begin now!*

But nothing began and the merry-go-round kept on turning.

For the first time in my life I began to struggle academically. The initial structured introductions and orientations of freshers' week gave way to large tracts of unaccounted-for time. I was expected to attend three lectures and one tutorial a week – and then what? Much as I had come to hate school and home, and missed neither, they had provided a predictable world, and routines and predictability can hold your world together even when everything else is falling apart. My organisational skills, the so-called executive skills, were poor, as they are for many people with autism spectrum disorders. I wasn't good at doing what I was supposed to do, often missing lectures or getting sidetracked by focussing on what interested me to the exclusion of all else. Told to get an essay in by nine o'clock tomorrow morning I could do it. Given a few vague weeks I was invariably late or sometimes the said essay would fail to materialise at all. Added to that, my anxiety levels at having to cope with being around so many new people, day and night, were going through the roof and I found I couldn't concentrate. It reflected in my work and I was hauled into my tutor's office a couple of times. Dr B was a very nice person who supported me a lot in the long run, but in those early days she clearly thought I was lazy and having too much of a good time at the taxpayers' expense. I lacked the words to explain that things were any different.

'You're not strong,' she told me. I stared at the floor, avoiding eye contact, which is, of course, a sure sign to make people think you're guilty. I read 'not strong' to mean that I was stupid, which is how I felt – stupid and inept and useless. My one certain point of identity and self-esteem was my ability to think and learn, and now I didn't even seem to have that. Like many other bright students before me, I had gone within the space of a few months from being a school wunderkind (albeit an odd one who hardly ever spoke), of whom words like 'brilliant' and 'genius' were randomly (and inaccurately) used, to just another run-of-the-mill work-shy student. I withdrew even more into my friendless, isolated world.

Anxiety made me restless. Alone in my hall of residence room at nights, the noisy social competents marauding in the corridors outside, I needed to block out the noise, the jar of human presences which invaded through my closed door. I took to walking around the streets and campus, pounding my feet in a rhythmic beat. I pounded deep into the nights, and if any kind of threat lurked out there, I was oblivious to it. I liked the quietness, the darkness, the purifying chill and the routine of counting, and it was another reason for never getting up in time for lectures in the morning.

One term in and I wasn't doing well.

Sitting alone in a lecture one day, I glanced around. It was an afternoon lecture so fairly well attended, most students having managed to drag themselves out of bed by 2pm. Of all of them, only I and another boy were sitting alone. He looked pale, unhappy and strained; maybe I looked the same. A few weeks later I saw him with a girlfriend. He looked relaxed and happy. I continued to sit in lectures alone.

But, so I reasoned, being in a minority of one, it was clearly I who had the problem. Culture in the form of music and songs and films bombarded us with the overriding importance of love and relationships all the time. The problem was I couldn't quite fathom it:

I can't live if living is without you.

Why?

Don't wanna be all by myself.

Why not?

If you leave me now, you'll take away the biggest part of me.

Uhh?

The very subject I studied – literature – was confirming again and again that all humans are motivated by relationships, that this is the be-all and end-all of human existence. *Reader, I married him and lived happily ever after* was the message the great Victorians all left stinging in your ear. Clearly the great writers knew something I didn't. But, then, everyone seemed to know something I didn't – even the solitary guy in the lecture theatre. Perhaps it was time to find out.

I observed the sexual mating games going on around me, grasped the theory and felt no particular need for the practice: surrendering what self you had to someone else made little sense, and why would you want to share time and space when being alone is the only time and space in which you are truly comfortable? How (and this most crucial of all) do you get rid of someone once you've let them in?

In the oestrogen-and-testosterone-fuelled atmosphere of the campus there was no shortage of willing male partners around and, after a lifetime closeted in a predominantly female environment, I was intrigued. I started to talk more and found that I preferred being around men, finding it less confusing. I enjoyed the earthier sense of humour, male banter and the comparative lack of emotional disclosures that I didn't know how to respond to. Whilst most of them were kind to me, it came at a price – I was young for my age, naive and hopeless at asserting myself. I'd never had much sense of myself as a physical being – maybe it goes with the autism territory where existence is predominantly on the inside. My biggest problem with my body was the attention other people gave to it – the stares, the sizing up, the desire to touch, possess, move close to it – and I was at the age and in a place where this was in full flow.

But I was curious and decided to find out more. And we all know what happened to the cat.

Young men, despite the media hype, are rarely good lovers. In the words of Hobbes, it was usually nasty, brutish and short. 'You were great,' said one, before rolling over and falling asleep, oblivious to the fact that I had stared at a damp stain on the ceiling and found pictures in it like a Rorschach blot throughout.

So that was what Shakespeare and Byron and Lawrence were talking about.

Date rape was common then, although the name had barely been invented. It happened on a regular basis and no one thought too much about it; you were just warned off certain men. Put simply, the word 'no' meant 'yes' or at least could be moulded into it by a process of nagging attrition and a bulge in a man's pair of jeans. Sometimes it didn't even take that.

Tim was a chemistry student, older than the rest of us by about three years, a self-appointed expert in all matters sexual. He had straight, blond hair and wore thick, square glasses which made him look a bit like Joe 90. He liked to educate me about the world and thought I needed to have a good sexual experience, appointing himself as the one to organise it. I wasn't attracted to him and sexual chemistry it wasn't. It was particularly nasty, brutish and short, and totally non-consensual.

'Don't worry, I'll make sure nothing happens,' he said, pushing me down on the bed. 'I'll stop in time.'

Something did happen.

As I grabbed my things and left, he sent me a parting piece of sex therapy counselling: 'You'll be fine, just try to relax a bit and enjoy it.'

On my 19th birthday I found out I was pregnant. Apart from the GP who arranged the termination for me, I told no one – including Tim. I went to the hospital alone and left alone at midday the next day. At 2pm on the same afternoon I sat alone in a lecture on Shakespeare's *Henry V*, determined that no one was ever going to get near me again.

I retreated back into myself, wondering why I had ever bothered to emerge in the first place.

In the final term of my first year, two strange things happened: I made friends and I got a permanent boyfriend.

The friends happened first. I had wandered into the kitchen at the end of my corridor, realising too late that someone was already in there (always my cue to go back and wait for them to leave). A small girl called Jasmine, with beautiful, mixed-race skin and shining, black hair, smiled at me and said, 'Hi.'

I felt, as always, trapped – unwilling to stay and too scared to leave. Oblivious, she talked – the kettle had just boiled if I wanted it, some git had stolen her milk again, it was pissing down outside and she had a lecture to go to.

Someone else came in. 'Hi, Marion, this is Sue.' Marion was small, Jewish, American. We were sitting at a table drinking coffee together and I was being invited to join a group of them going to see a film that night.

And that's how it happened. I became, if only peripherally, part of a group of six girls. I was invited to things, people talked to me and, strangest of all, most of them seemed to like me. My naivety and lack of social knowhow were viewed with a kind of tolerant affection: I was different but not the freak I had assumed myself to be. I seemed to have made friends by default and the fact that I remained partly outside of the group was neither here nor there. I could dip into it if I wanted or stay out if I didn't; I'd got my foot in the door, and if one foot was still outside, it made retreat, should it be necessary, easier, and in my world an escape route was always a primary requirement. On that basis, I could risk making friends.

Then the boyfriend happened.

David was running a free Hebrew class. I attended because I liked learning languages, not out of any intention to meet someone. He was orthodox Jewish, not long out of a Yeshiva and I was Catholic, not long out of a convent school. One night he offered to walk me home. Walking home in the dark, we slipped into an easy conversation. I felt comfortable with him, perhaps because we were, in our different ways, both outsiders and perhaps because somewhere along the way I had acquired some of the social skills I needed to get by and developed a better social tolerance when it came to being around others. Next day there was a bunch of red roses in my pigeon hole and a card asking if he could see me again. A few months later we moved in together. I seemed to have arrived at normality. The only trouble was it was hell.

My live-in relationship with David lasted approximately six months. Being in a relationship, let alone living with someone, was seriously over-ambitious. I didn't understand what relationships, never mind shared living, entailed, nor how much my inner survival depended on privacy and long periods alone. Simple things like telling someone where I was going or having to make a joint decision didn't make sense. Sharing toothpaste, a duvet, a front-door key left me feeling that my private self was invaded and overwhelmed. Nor did I understand why David felt he had to spend time with his family and co-religionists when my prime motivation in coming to university had been to escape all of that. When he disappeared off to the synagogue on Saturdays or to festivals, I remained alone in the flat, with no sense of anyone else to go to and conscious that, as a non-Jew, I would never be welcomed into his wider social circle, even if I had been capable of voluntarily entering it. I responded by withdrawing into myself, a shutting down which was also an angry protest at feeling forced to surrender who I was to an incomprehensible social code. Again, it came down to risk of annihilation around others or survival alone. He was patient, caring and forgiving; I was stroppy, miserable and silent. At 19, I had an overwhelming feeling that I had waited too late or too long to ever join in the world around me, to ever understand what seemed so natural to everyone else.

In the end I moved out, convinced of my own failure and that I was never going to join the ranks of the normal. It never occurred to me that I would make more friends or get into a relationship again. In my reasoning, it all happened by chance: you were in a certain place at a certain time and someone spoke to you and wanted to know you. That this was a two-way process or one that could generate from within was beyond my grasp. I was back alone, and that was clearly where the universe had deemed I belonged; it was pure hubris to expect anything more.

I relocated back to an ugly high-rise hall of residence, hating and despising myself for what I perceived as my failure, but also raging against what I perceived as the world's unfairness, the excluding and exclusive world which was open to some but not to others like me. Turning outwards towards the world had proved too painful and difficult. With the anger of the dispossessed, I turned my back on it in fury and disgust and defeat, turned back to the only world I knew how to live in.

It was an *If you can't beat them, join them* response, except I wasn't joining anyone. I was about to go more solo than I ever had before.

2

hungry

'Are you all right?'

For God's sake, get up! I was ordering myself, but for some reason I couldn't obey the order. I was lying on the floor in the foyer of the university main library, my body twitching whilst I furiously cursed it and ordered it to obey, to stand up and walk.

'Are you all right?' someone asked again.

'I'm OK,' I snapped impatiently at the voice above me, to the faces I couldn't see because my vision was blocked out by racing lights and stars. I forced myself up on to my knees and prepared to stand. A hand pressed down on the bones of my shoulder.

'Stay where you are.' Clearly I was under arrest.

'I'm all right.' That was the confession they were after, wasn't it?

My eyes came into focus. A woman was squatting down beside me; it was her hand on my shoulder. She was looking at it as if she couldn't quite believe what she was feeling. A small group had gathered around me. I cringed with embarrassment.

No one believed my confession. Despite my protests, I was ferried to the medical centre.

It had all started simply enough: I just decided to stop eating. I lived alone in a self-catering hall and no one was checking up on whether I ate or not. There was no angst about being fat, about fitting in with media stereotypes; no one had made disparaging comments about how I looked. It was just that one day I was eating and the next day I wasn't. At least not much – meals were off the menu; a few calories here and there would suffice instead. I thought it would all last a few weeks, that it was nothing more than a brief, angry hunger strike at the world I felt so excluded from, that it would all be over by Christmas, but, without knowing it, I had signed up for nearly a decade of disordered eating.

And in the beginning everything was better, much better. Suddenly I had a reason to get up in the morning: there was so much starving to get through. My days had changed from a floating unstructured mess into a routine whose purpose was so overriding that any deviation from it seemed worse than death. I was up at dawn every day, fuelled by a cup of tea with three teaspoons of skimmed milk, biking up to the library and doing two or three rounds of the campus to get rid of the calories in the milk before I settled into an eight-hour day of reading. And whilst I was at it, I might as well just do four or five more rounds before I started in case there were any calories from the day before to work off. And then again, if the last circuit had been a bit slow, I might as well throw in another one just for good measure and to offset any excess calories I might eat during the day. I threw off the self-pity of depression and decided I was going to fulfil my academic potential and get a first-class degree; there was no time for a social life, no time for friends, no time for relationships, no time to eat. I was on a serious mission.

I entered the anorexic world as I entered all obsessions: excluding and mono-focussed, protected from and holding the world at bay. Turning on my body took me deeper and deeper inside myself, and as I physically receded, my autistic self expanded. With hunger came the licence I wanted not to talk, not to smile, to stay away from everyone lest (God forbid) they might lead me into the temptation of eating. And initially hunger seemed a small price to pay for such benefits. I began to live in a blunted, frozen space, and because hunger protected me from the confusion and terror of the social world, I embraced it. And because I embraced it, it enslaved me.

My world was now reduced wholly to myself: professional calorie counter, exercise fanatic, Skinniest Girl on the Planet in the making. I counted calories down to the toothpaste on the toothbrush, ate cereal (when I ate) with water and endlessly read cookbooks, memorised recipes, looked at food on shop shelves in a *look but don't touch* world that I had managed to conquer. As the starvation progressed, I began to see things in technicolour, heard more acutely and smelled so keenly that the scent of food could suspend me in amazing wonder long after it had passed away. I watched this surprising new world unfold, convinced that I had reached a higher state of being that was locked off to mere mortals. And there is nothing like being able to eat less than everyone else to give you a sense of moral superiority: I regarded those around me with pitying contempt. I was no longer a social failure because I had no need of society at all. I was safe in my vastly superior, cut-off world.

Incidences of recorded anorexia were significantly fewer then: there were no anorexic websites to swap tips on, and feminist theory had only just decided that fat was a feminist issue. I felt I had arrived at my own unique solution – I was on to something good and nobody else was. (I did in fact meet one other anorexic girl at university. We circled round each other like hissing cats fighting over a fish bone. She glared enviously at my hands which looked like claws, whilst I stared at her protruding hip bones and decided that her bum was bigger than mine anyway.)

Ironically, prior to anorexia I had never had any particular issues around weight, but once in its snare I could check my weight up to ten times in a day, looking in terror at the scales which I felt could literally destroy me by ounces gained or make me ecstatic with ounces lost. Looking in the full-length mirror, I noted my emerging skeleton with narcissistic pleasure: my protruding rib cage, the hip bones which could hold a ruler, the knees that were wider than my thighs, all testimony to what had been the hardest struggle in my life. I was starting to get somewhere at last, but in this dysmorphic world I could still see myself as fat. I wasn't *there* yet, wherever *there* was – some ever-receding zero point on the scales. There was always more flesh to lose. Besides, I felt incredibly heavy. Every step I took began to require a massive effort, a dogged lifting of one leg in front of the other, my knee bones clanking as I did so. It would take me several years to realise that the bars of my rib cage were as symptomatic of a prison as of a bid for freedom from the world, and that I was both my own jailor and my own prisoner.

Standing in front of the mirror one day, a movement from outside caught my eye.

Sodding moggy!

I banged furiously on the bedsit window. The scrawny cat nearly jumped out of its ginger pelt. It looked up from where it was scavenging in the dustbin, rigid, as if ready to bound off over the neighbouring fence.

I banged again until it ran away, leaving the scraps in the bin. That bin was my territory now. I had moved into the bedsit during the summer vacation, an upstairs one where I lived alone, studiously avoiding the neighbours. But I knew exactly what they ate. I watched daily from the upstairs window as they threw away the remnants of their meals in the dustbin – the crusts of bread, carrot peelings, scraps of meat and fish, peppered by cigarette ash from an ashtray. How could anyone possibly throw away food when they had full permission to eat it? Lacking that permission, I watched the appalling waste go on beneath me, fascinated and repelled. Just sometimes I broke rank, driven by that nuisance called hunger to go down and stare inside the bin when no one was about. Once or twice I was tempted to reach into the bin and eat in my desperate need to taste again, to remember the texture of food, to quieten the ever-gnawing hunger. No matter that it tasted of grit: carrot peelings peppered with cigarette ash – a kind of *carotte au poivre* in the strange anorexic gastronomy – filled a gaping emptiness.

And the truth was I *was* gapingly empty and had felt so for years. Anorexia provided an apt metaphorical mirroring of my inner state of aching, empty aloneness that only the truly excluded can know. Hunger was a symbolic externalisation of my inability to nurture or be nurtured socially: I could not reach out and I could not take in. But in my case – and here is perhaps the tragedy of autism, a pervasive development disorder that affects you for life – I was never going to be filled – at least not by that external world, by that species of which I was both a member and from which I seemed so catastrophically cut off. Back then, however, I did not fully realise this. On some level the delusion persisted that one day it would all just work out in the wash, that I would graduate as a fully paid-up member of the human race; I would find and read the book that would show me the way. Meanwhile, I went hungry.

Ironically, I read and forgot more in those years than at any time before or since. During my long daily stints alone at the library, feeling permanently cold, my seat bones and back bones pressing painfully into the chair, I worked out a scheme: for every two pages I read, I could eat a sweet (chocolate limes were my favourites). I calculated how much reading I could get through on the average-size bag. It came to about 40 pages, which was too many chocolate limes (or whatever it was) at × number of calories per sweet (carefully looked up in my slimmer's book of calorie counting). I upped my reading: three pages per sweet. It was still far too many, I knew, but all this reading had to be got through somehow, as anyone who has ever tackled the eighteenth-century novel will know. In its way this was quite a good plan, but I found myself skimming over words, taking nothing in just to get to the next part of my rations. Hunger and learning don't go together: something was persistently urging me to keep moving and, like my body, my brain was craving physical sustenance. I accepted the physical discomforts willingly enough – after all, I had put them there – but when my mind didn't seem to be functioning properly, it was worrying.

One day Jasmine, who I hadn't seen for a long time, found me reading in the library and wandered up casually. I saw her approach out of the corner of my eye and inwardly groaned –

I hadn't the energy to deal with people any more, even if I'd wanted to in the first place.

'How's things?' she asked, smiling from that normal world where people smiled.

'Great,' I said, noting for the first time that her round face had a double chin.

'You look different.'

I nodded. 'New haircut.'

She stared at me hard. 'No, it's something else. Your face looks different.'

Despite retreating into multiple layers of very loose clothing to combat the ever-present cold, I couldn't hide the fact that my cheekbones were sticking out and my hands resembled bird claws. She gave me a strange look and shrugged. 'I'll just take one of these.'

I watched as three pages of reading disappeared into her mouth.

Fucking bitch!

I thought it rather than said it. There are no worse crimes than to come between an anorexic and their set rations – bar none. I don't think I ever spoke to Jasmine again, but, then, friends would only have been a hindrance in my quest to exit society altogether.

I got away with it until I weighed less than six stone. For some weeks I had been crashing to my knees every time I got up in the morning after a night spent in the restless agitation that compelled me to keep moving, to endlessly toss and turn whilst I tried to find a comfortable position for my protruding bones on the mattress. I accepted the crashing to my knees when I first stood up and began to anticipate the lights flashing in my head that accompanied it – in my grander scheme it seemed like a small price to pay. Lately, though, I also seemed to be experiencing some kind of fitting which saw me twitching on the ground, conscious of everything but unable to respond and furious with myself because of it. When the fit was over, I would drag myself to my knees and force myself to stand up on shaking legs before the day subsumed me in the manic exercise and dieting that had become my life.

That was how I ended up in the doctor's office.

The doctor who saw me took my weight and shone a torch in my eyes. He was horseshoe bald, had protruding eyes behind rimless glasses and spoke in a public-school accent. He asked me when I'd last eaten.

'Lunchtime.'

Actually, it was at breakfast: the white of an otherwise discarded boiled egg. Ten calories. Plus salt. Plus a teaspoon of mustard. And then there was that skimmed milk in the tea. The calories were all adding up horribly. I made a mental note to myself to try just three-quarters of a teaspoon of mustard next time.

'How long's this been going on for?'

'What?' I shot him a dirty look.

'Heard of anorexia nervosa?' he said. I had. It was called the slimmer's disease, which I knew was rubbish because I wasn't trying to be slim; I was trying to starve myself out of this oh-too-mortal world around me. This doctor clearly didn't understand that. I felt sorry for him.

'Are you doing it to be thin?' he demanded, taking my blood pressure. I noted with a self-satisfied smirk that he had had to find a smaller, child-size cuff to fit round my emaciated upper arm – proof that I was heading in the right direction.

'Doing what?' I glared at him defensively. It was none of his damn business.

He gave me a long lecture on why eating was essential to any living organism, why I was no different from anyone else in that respect, how I could expect to die if I didn't change my ways. It washed over me as I listened with the superiority of the enlightened. I sensed that he didn't like me or what I was doing. No matter: it was mutual.

'Do you think you're immortal?' he asked suddenly, snapping my attention away from a picture I'd been staring at on the wall, of a gundog with a dead pheasant in its mouth. I frog-marched my mind back from thoughts of roast pheasant, potatoes, gravy, vegetables…all of it now far beyond my wildest dreams.

'I need to see you again next week.'

I agreed to come back to have my weight taken, to eat more, to speak to the university counsellor. I'd have agreed to anything to get out of that goddamn doctor's office.

I stayed the right side of hospital admission, aided by the litany of lies that trip so easily out of an anorexic's otherwise firmly closed mouth – *Yes, I am eating more*; *No, I don't want to lose weight*; *Yes, it's great to feel normal again* – and the behaviours that back it up: the glasses of water consumed before doctor's visits, the weights in the pockets, the puking after meals consumed in front of others, the laxative abuse. In my usual obsessive way, I had read all about anorexia to the point where

I knew more about it than the medical professionals I came into contact with. I knew what to say to set them on a false course and I knew what to do to remain on my single-minded track. And as an adult – nominally at least, though I still felt myself to be, and probably was in many ways, much younger than my peer group – I could do what I wanted. No one was going to stop me.

Responses to my receding person varied from the unhelpful: *You're as bad as a drug addict* (doctor), the sympathetic: *Whatever you're doing it for, you're doing it for a good reason* (counsellor), to the terrifying: *I've brought you something to eat* (friend). My family of origin, with whom I had increasingly little contact, were not made aware of it. My tutor and the lecturers in the English department were kind and accommodating, making the excuses for me that I could not make for myself. The university psychologist fed back to them that I had been underperforming academically for a reason and that I was in fact unusually bright but 'obviously quite disturbed'.

It was around this time that the term 'autism' was first mentioned to me. A healthcare professional commented in passing that some of my behaviour seemed quite autistic. Autism then was largely regarded as a form of childhood psychosis; medical opinion was still dominated by the thinking of Bruno Bettelheim whose notorious *Refrigerator Mothers* supposedly sent their offspring retreating back into the freezer never to emerge again (mothers were also largely blamed for causing anorexia then too). As I was not a child, was not psychotic and didn't have any learning difficulties, I clearly didn't fit the bill, and Asperger's, with its higher intelligence profile, had barely been heard of. The causes of the anorexia became subsumed in dealing with the symptoms, but even then I probably knew that something was going on deep inside me which no amount of therapy would ever cure.

A year later I got my degree (not a brilliant one but reasonable under the circumstances). No one came to watch me graduate and I invited no one, my relationship with family having progressively disintegrated since I left home to the point of non-existence. I spent graduation day alone in a bedsit reading Samuel Beckett's *Murphy*. That at least made me laugh but not much else did at that time. On some level I wanted to connect with the world around me, the world I felt hopelessly excluded from but was too afraid and frozen to reach out to. Hunger is hell and I wanted someone to give me permission to eat again, but no one seemed to have that much authority. I had been in therapy for some time but there had been little progress: I was locked into silence, into a terrified autistic prison; if I communicated with the world, it was through my hunger and increasingly through that other silent language of self-harm. The cuts on my arms remained largely hidden, but desperation was leading me to smash my head against walls and tables in what seemed to be a bid to break out of my locked-in world, a literal attempt to break out of the frozen silence that trapped me, with the predictable result that my face was often a mass of colourful bruises. I took two overdoses and was given a stark choice: voluntary external patient at a psychiatric therapeutic community or be sectioned. I chose the former.

The therapeutic community ran daily at an old-style county lunatic asylum sited on the borders of two counties (a throwback to the times when the counties' insane were banished out of sight). The sprawling, old red-brick asylum was a self-contained world, with its own laundry, cricket pitch and morgue. On my first day, as I wandered through the huge porch entrance and down a maze of corridors in search of the outpatients' department, I looked around and shuddered. The morgue in particular suggested that once you were in, there was only one way out – even if you could watch the odd game of cricket along the way. From behind a locked door on one of the wards I could hear harrowing screams echoing down the endless linoleum-floored corridors, with their stench of cleaning fluid and excrement. It was Dante's final circle. I prepared to abandon hope.

'You want the building outside,' a male cleaner told me when I plucked up the courage to ask where to go. That was a relief.

'It's down there,' he added. I thanked my present-day Virgil and hastily broke out of the asylum.

There were about 20 patients at the therapeutic community and the day was structured around small-group therapy sessions, large-group sessions and a slot for psychodrama. There were three written rules in the community: No Drugs, No Violence and No Sex. There was a fourth unwritten rule: All Therapists are Gods.

Although you could have wiped the floor with my self-esteem at that time, I never reached a point where I would unquestioningly defer to authority or not question what I thought was questionable. It did not make me popular – with the therapists at least. When one particularly nasty one, with a penchant for labelling anyone who dared to question her, announced to the main group of patients and therapists that I was a 'yes-but girl' for suggesting that there might be an alternative viewpoint to what she had said, I asked her in my sweetest possible manner, 'And where did you do your training – Dachau?' It struck me as a system whose purpose was to break you down, to remould you in someone else's image, and the sad thing was most of the patients were too cowed to do anything but accept it.

The community was a strange, inward-looking world. In the absence of any proper or sensible topic of conversation, a ludicrous array of pseudo-Freudian interpretations were thrown out randomly as received wisdom. Norms became pathologised and the pathological regarded as normal. A patient heading off to the toilet in the middle of a group was rich fodder:

'Sean, why are you going to the toilet right now?'

'I need a piss.'

'Shall we talk about that?'

'I just need a piss.'

'Sometimes we do things to avoid dealing with what's uncomfortable. I'd urge you to try to stay with it.'

This during a discussion of who was responsible for the dirty cups in the sink. Sean shot me a glance which said, *What's more uncomfortable than sitting here desperate for a piss?* In the meantime, another patient, who from time to time thought he was Jesus, quoted Isaiah at us, his gathered disciples, and went ignored.

Sean was my silent ally. We escaped together at lunchtime to the river which ran by the edge of the asylum grounds, Sean to smoke a joint, me to avoid eating. We didn't talk much, mostly lying on our backs on the grass and looking up into the blue sky of a rare summer heatwave – if I'd been feeling anything other than hopelessly lost and alone and depressed, I might have found it quite beautiful. Sean had a history of drug abuse which had led to a psychotic breakdown and depression. He had dropped out of school at 16. In many ways we were opposites, but we found each other easy to be around. Sean didn't speak much, but when he did it was to the point:

'It's shit here, innit?'

'Yeah.'

Unsurprisingly, I didn't last long at the community. There was no way I could cope with the intensity of group situations, and I spent more time staying away than actually being there. I was accused of acting out, being uncooperative, failing to comply, and before I left I acquired a few more labels. The discharge report which followed a two-week absence observed: 'She seems afraid of belonging to any group.' That was true: I just didn't do groups – they caused me to fragment into too many pieces – but I was no closer to understanding what was wrong. I patently wasn't 'mad' (though in some ways I would have welcomed such a diagnosis because then at least I would have known what I was dealing with), but I knew I wasn't exactly 'normal' either. I experienced the world – the human social world – differently. The social species continued to baffle me.

I left the so-called therapeutic community with a lifetime of abiding scepticism of the power structure of psychiatry and therapy, but in other ways it had proved a wake-up call. I realised I needed to take control of my own life, to find a way in the outside world rather than retreat into the twilight world of a hospital and the abdication of responsibility for myself to dubious others with a private agenda and more ready-made labels than a canning factory.

I began to appraise my eating problems more rationally: in anorexia, the body is used to doing the talking, and to talk loudly enough requires a supreme effort – it is called starvation. I had been using my body as an indirect way of speaking to the world because I felt verbally locked in on myself. But I was out in the world on my own now, and was anyone really listening anyway? And if they were, did they know what they were listening to?

It was also becoming apparent to me that anorexia is shot through with contradictions: as you become lighter, you feel so heavy that you can't move; you get thin and you feel permanently fat; you have a belief that this is the way to nirvana, but no matter how much you give (and you can give everything) you will never arrive; you convince yourself that you are on a higher plane and spend your days drooling over dustbin scraps or puking up in public toilets.

In other words, you can't win. It beats you every time and it will race you to the death if you let it.

Slowly coming to this realisation, I began to eat more normally again. It was a three-steps-forward-and-two-steps-back process. Anorexia mutated into a protracted phase of bulimia which I found relatively easier – I could, so to speak, eat *ad nauseam*, have my cake and eat it. I became caught for several years in the binge–purge rituals which also helped to provide a barrier to the outside world, but I could still function in it better than I had been able to do with anorexia. In all, it was a battle that took more than a decade to resolve wholly. Ultimately, I think the eating disorders stopped because I got bored with it all – the obsession had run its course and there were other things I wanted to focus on. I didn't want to make starvation my life's work and I didn't want to spend hours paying homage on my knees to the porcelain god in the bathroom. Nor did I want to go for half measures, caught between starvation and sustenance, living some pointless half-life for no real purpose other than to make some obtuse point to a world that wasn't listening anyway – there were better things to do.

Curiosity got the better of me again and this time it didn't kill me.

3

homeless

It was the mid-80s economic crisis and for the first time graduates were graduating straight on to the dole queue. I joined them, embarrassed but not sure what to do. University had held me for three years and now I was out on my own, but I had no sense of having a place in the world which made making my way in it decidedly tricky. The automatic sliding doors which came between me and the world continued to cut me off, leaving me adrift. I didn't really know what career I wanted. I harboured vague notions of becoming a journalist but lacked the social confidence and social contacts to go out and do it. Like so much else, it seemed to belong to other people in their world, not me in my strange closed-off one.

Eventually, when I had some degree of control over my eating and was functional (if undernourished), I decided it was time to get some life experience. I had had enough of books and reading for a while; I wanted to find out about the *real thing*. Still convinced of my outsider status, I sought the least glamorous option I could and worked as a volunteer amongst London's street homeless.

I worked for several months in a night shelter and at the rough sleeping sites of King's Cross, Piccadilly, Charing Cross, Waterloo and other places where the destitute, the alcoholics, drug addicts, the mentally ill and criminals found refuge. The work mainly involved providing food and basic shelter, with an ethos of inclusion and acceptance for the most marginalised of people. I learned about the language of the streets, the conning and conniving needed for daily survival, the brutal dog-eat-dog world, the tragedies that underpinned so many broken lives and the cold, hard indifference that is London when you are down and out. Curiously, I felt more at home there than I ever had in a lecture theatre at university.

Cardboard City was the name given to the homeless community living under the arches of Waterloo railway station although it was also applied loosely to most of the larger rough-sleeping sites around London. In the mid-80s an estimated 200 homeless people, mainly men, slept on the street at Waterloo in cardboard boxes, that last pathetic bastion against the coldness of the pavement. The majority of the cardboard citizens then were street drinkers; a few of the older ones still drank meths (methylated spirits). Heroin and Aids had just started to rear their hideous twin-hydra heads. The heroin users tended to be younger men, openly despised by the street drinkers who operated a strict hierarchy. The few women who ended up there were mostly alcoholics and the mentally ill who survived by street prostitution. Many of the drinkers were Irish who had migrated to London in search of work, to be greeted by that most infamous of welcomes on some of the bed-and-breakfast boarding houses where they might have gone: *No dogs, no wogs, no Irish*. Under the arches of Charing Cross one wag had written up a town-twinning sign, appropriately enough on cardboard: *Cardboard City twinned with Vatican City* – it wasn't that uncommon for the Irish street drinkers to have rosary beads in one pocket and a bottle of White Lightning in the other. One year, I'm told, someone managed to 'arrange' a Christmas tree on the streets for the annual festivities. It was gallows humour and it needed to be. Several times a day, soup vans did the rounds with handouts. Social workers sometimes dropped by to pick up the most needy. Sometimes it was too late; a few unfortunate souls lived and died on the streets.

Initially I found it difficult to get on with some of my co-workers, but I was always tolerated because I seemed to have a natural gift for getting on with life's outcasts, perhaps because I was such a marginal person myself. I would prefer to sit and talk to them rather than talk to my 'peer group' of young graduates, all of whom seemed to have comfortable middle-class homes behind them to run to in times of need. My colleagues objected that I read rather than talked – clearly that was a social sin – but as they got to know me, most of them accepted me as I was – a bit odd but decent enough. I was known for being clever and speaking my mind, which did not endear me to the boss of the charity I worked for. I have always struggled with authority figures.

When the stress of working with others overcame me, as it would do again and again in my working life, I decided it was time to quit. I left and with the job went the roof over my head. Assuming no one would mind, I stayed temporarily in the house of my co-workers, and no one did object until it was filtered down to me that the boss wasn't happy about it. Clearly I was not welcome. It was probably assumed that somewhere a home awaited me, with clean sheets, a washing machine and three meals a day. I never thought to tell anyone that I had no home

I wanted to go back to, that I felt I could only retain a sense of myself intact if I stayed alone, that concepts such as home and family threatened engulfment and psychological disintegration. Perhaps it was just one of those many occasions where a simple explanation and a request for help would have rescued me, but I couldn't explain and I found it all but impossible to ask for help. This was so ingrained in me that I gravitated in a dazed state towards what I knew – Cardboard City.

It was summer. I had a sleeping bag. My few other possessions had been abandoned at the workers' house. Yesterday I had been a young middle-class graduate; today I was on the streets and I looked back at the world I had left with new eyes – overnight it had become out of my reach, a gigantic divide had come between me and it. And yet, in my autistic world, I wasn't overly surprised. The world that others inhabited had always seemed out of reach; I had at best a toehold in it. Lacking any sense of a fixed social identity meant I could segue effortlessly between different states and different people; it was that which made me end up in places like this, that which enabled me to go through bizarre and often dangerous situations without too many questions. It wasn't just the absence of a safety net beneath me, that solidly woven mesh of family and friendships and connections that is sometimes so tight it can seem as solid as the ground itself; it was the inability to create one, to emerge from my inner autistic world to form the social connections that would catch me if I fell, breaking the crash landings which so often left me lying on the earth, licking my wounds and vowing never again, until next time when I'd spring back like a cartoon rabbit for whatever else life threw at me or I inadvertently created.

It was early evening when I arrived beneath the Charing Cross arches. I went there because it was the one place where I felt I might find people who would 'take me in', if you can call sharing a patch on a pavement being 'taken in'. As luck would have it, and as I had hoped, some of the street dwellers I had known from the early-morning soup run saw me. I had always got on well with them and they appeared to have a soft spot for me. It was Jimmy who spotted me first, from where he was lounging on the pavement with a bottle of sherry and his dog, Patch, an indeterminate mongrel who was pure black and had no evidence of any patch, lying beside him. Quite a few of the street dwellers had dogs – they were often their only companion as well as a source of protection and a wonderful begging asset. Having a dog usually kept someone on the streets because none of the hostels would take them, but people like Jimmy would not part with their dogs for anyone, preferring to remain on the street. It was a reasoning I could understand.

Jimmy had come to England from Kerry in the 1950s as a migrant worker. He had worked as a navvy, building the infrastructure of the roadways on which so much of England depended, but, unable to find somewhere permanent to stay and increasingly turning to alcohol, he had been homeless for many years. He was regarded as something of a leader amongst the London dossers (as they called themselves) and in his more drunken moments he sometimes roared out that he was 'King of the dossers', in the surprisingly hierarchical world of the streets. I liked Jimmy. He was verbally adroit, funny and always appreciative of life's small mercies, such as a 10p found on the pavement or a food donation of rice pudding. When he saw me standing alone under the arches, he called to me: 'Well, hello, Suzy. Is it the soup run you're on tonight?'

I told him briefly what had happened, how I couldn't stay where I was any more.

'Fucking bastards!' he said.

'Mmm.' I couldn't bring myself to say it, but that was pretty much what I was thinking and feeling about the situation too.

We shared roll-up cigarettes.

'Here, let me do that for you – Jaysus, it looks like the wacky baccy.' No matter how much I practised, I could never produce a decent roll-up. Jimmy rolled it with expert nicotine-brown fingers which shook slightly. He smelled, as did everyone, of alcohol and the streets. I expected I would do soon too.

'Now then,' he said after a few puffs and a swig from his Irish Cream Sherry bottle, 'where are you going to be staying tonight?'

I shrugged. 'Nowhere.'

'Will your mammy and daddy not be wondering where you are?' In different circumstances I might have laughed. To Jimmy, I was a child, a part of that other world which he and I, in our very different ways, were excluded from.

'I haven't got anywhere to go,' I said. 'I'll have to stay here.'

He drew in his breath. 'It's no place for a young lady.' Then, looking around, he called out to Mac. Mac was perhaps in his fifties; his grizzled beard and wild long hair made it difficult to tell. He wore a raincoat of indeterminate colour (the accrued colours of many years of living in it) tied with a string belt. 'We'll be wanting to keep this young lady safe tonight. See she gets a safe place.'

Between them, these men of the street arranged for me to place my sleeping bag behind a concrete pillar where I was effectively hidden from view. They brought me a sandwich and coffee from the soup van when it arrived; they slept outside on cardboard boxes with meagre blankets and told everyone else to leave me alone. They were nature's perfect gentlemen, excluded from society and therefore not merely being kind because of societal expectations – they were naturally kind.

The street was cold and hard and noisy. The night was broken by scuffles, fights, the crazy ramblings of the mentally ill, a former concentration camp prisoner jumping to attention by her cardboard bed as the 'camp commandant' conducted a roll call which had haunted her nightmares for decades. About 3am the solitary mournful sound of a mouth organ serenaded the 'sleepers' with an Irish ballad and then was silenced by a Glaswegian roar of 'See you – shut the fuck up!' At five o'clock word went up that the street cleaners were coming, sending the rough sleepers scarpering as machines sprayed the pavement, those too drunk or asleep to move receiving a brutal shower of cold water in the already freezing night.

Some years previously I had read Orwell's *A Clergyman's Daughter* which contains a brilliant scene of a sheltered young woman spending a night on the street. It flickered through my brain as I lurched in and out of sleep. In the book, Dorothy, the heroine, finds the cold hardest to deal with. Nothing much had changed: it was the cold and consequent sleeplessness, the 4am low point, that make you feel you would give anything just to be warm and to sleep properly again, that are the curse of the street dweller. Towards dawn I began to remember the prisoner scene in *War and Peace* where Pierre Bezukhov bivouacs by a fire at night in a frozen Russian winter, alternately turning sides, half warm, half frozen. A fire would have been nice. No wonder the men drank to cope with it.

I spent several nights on the streets at Charing Cross that summer. I was young enough and resilient enough to find it an interesting if not particularly pleasant experience. The lens of fiction had, as always, helped me to filter the experience, to find a context and a point of comparison. In the absence of human contact this was to prove useful again and again. I might be alone but I knew the stories of others who had been there – it is one of the saving graces of fiction.

I had been lucky to be looked after by Jimmy and Patch and the crew, and, unlike Jimmy and the crew, I had my middle-class education to get me out of it, although initially, in my naivety and ignorance, I was stymied. Where do you go to in London when you are (a) homeless and (b) penniless? It was Jimmy who brought me to the attention of one of the outreach social workers who came once a week with one of the soup vans. They recommended a hostel for homeless women near Euston and advised me about claiming dole money as a homeless person.

The hostel was hidden away in a quiet square near Great Ormond Street Children's Hospital. A lovely large Jamaican lady called Deena admitted me. Hearing my educated voice, she gave me a sideways glance but asked no questions. She was kind to me and I had a bed and a roof over my head and two meals a day if my intermittent anorexia permitted me to eat. There was a communal area, a dining room with a drinks machine that was as liable to dispense cockroaches as coffee, and several dormitories and shared rooms.

The hostel was home to aging prostitutes, a lady who had moved up from south Wales to be nearer to her husband who was doing a stretch in Pentonville, the mad, the sad and the dispossessed. And me. I wasn't sure which category I fitted; I was the youngest by an average of 20 years and, because I was small and quiet and fairly polite, I managed to avoid confrontation on the whole. The only person my age, an enormous black girl from Kenya who repeated herself a lot, singled me out as an ally. She told me she was waiting to be admitted to a therapeutic community and that she heard voices – I hoped they were more benevolent than those of some of the older residents who never lost an opportunity to tell her to 'piss off back to your own country'. On the other hand, Agneta, who had come from Poland after the War, was adept at telling me to get out of her room in a mix of angry Polish and broken English. Rumour had it that she had been a slave labourer in Germany. Eventually, my presence in 'her' room led her to storm off in fury. I then had the room to myself, which made me happy.

I usually waited till late at night before I came down to sit in the communal living room to read in the warmth. By then most people had gone to bed and the only other person who stayed up late was Elsie. Elsie had an unassuming kindness and gentleness about her that made her easy to be around. Born in a slum in the East End, her family home had been bombed during the Second World War. She talked to me about her life as a Londoner working in a garment factory (she had never been out of the capital city in her entire life). As a pensioner, she had been housed in a sheltered housing block.

'It was loverly,' she said in an accent uncannily close to Eliza Doolittle's. All Elsie wanted was a room somewhere as well. 'I 'ad me own barfroom and an inside toilet – never 'ad that before. But then I 'ad problems wiv me neighbours.'

Elsie wasn't sure which one of them it was who had been coming through her walls, spying on her when she was asleep. She felt she couldn't be sure and therefore it was better not to stay there. Her social worker had helped her move here. Where she would go in the future, Elsie did not know.

After the past few months I seemed to be depressed. I spent hours lying in bed, looking at the wall. At other times I sat in cafés, eking out cups of coffee to fill the hours (it was an old eating-disorder habit – I could make a piece of bread last for hours). Being homeless is nothing if not boring. Then I discovered the massive library near Euston Station.

I had always loved libraries almost to the point of veneration: they were an external manifestation of all the internal possibilities of my mind. Heaven, if it existed, would be the ultimate, never-ending library. I had been in libraries from before I could read; my mother used to leave my older sisters and me in the children's section of the local one whilst she, also an obsessive reader, perused the adult section. It was free childcare before it was even invented – and what fabulous childcare it was! Under the eye of the children's librarian (who let me play with her book stamp in a pre-computerised library world), I looked for hours at picture books and learned by heart the colours and shapes and order of the book spines on the shelves. It was a love affair from day one.

Once I had learned to read, there was no stopping me and I often had four books on the go at the same time, stashed somewhere around the house in case I finished one, a stage which always left me in a rising panic about where the next one was going to come from. By the time I was 14 and able to graduate into the adult library section, I didn't just see books on shelves, I saw infinity. The endless possibilities of learning opened up for me on those shelves, each slender book spine holding a world within itself which could lead to another world and another and another… I began to visit the library daily after school; sitting under the roof dome reading, with the sun's rays streaming down on to the desk in front of me, I could turn my back on the mundane world. I had found a better one.

The reading and knowledge I gleaned from books were to become the portable currency that I carried with me throughout my life, an inner richness which no one could take away. Each book I read represented for me a coin in my internal treasure chest – and the supply was infinite. Whilst my cut-off state meant that I could never hope to possess in actual terms what most of my contemporaries did, on a good day the value that I carried inside me often made me feel like the richest person alive. And so it was here – homeless, friendless, alone and depressed, I still had wealth inside me and there was more waiting without.

The modern edifice near Euston was a homecoming in a homeless world. I couldn't actually join this library because I was technically classed as being of No Fixed Abode, or NFA – another sideways glance came my way when the librarian behind the desk found this out. She looked at me in the snotty way of librarians who suspect your hands might make *their* books dirty. No matter: I could read the books there all day. And I read obsessively.

I made the daily trek down the road towards Euston and spent my days there and as much of the evening as I could. The library was a popular refuge for homeless people. It was a shelter for the day, somewhere to sit down, and if you weren't obviously drunk and didn't make a racket, you were tolerated. Many took the opportunity to sleep, doubtless a result of the cold, sleep-deprived streets or stations where they had spent the night. Every so often a middle-aged Jamaican man would come round and in a loud voice tell the grizzled, grimy sleepers to wake up:

'No sleeping in the library. That's how we nearly lost the war against Hitler.'

Probably some of them wondered what kind of world all the fighting had been for.

Meanwhile, I kept my head down and read about my latest obsession: abnormal psychology. I read Freud, Jung, Klein and Laing in search of answers, to know why my life seemed always to go so horribly wrong. I didn't find any. I scoured the *Diagnostic and Statistical Manual of Mental Disorders* from cover to cover and decided that I probably had a touch of everything in it, but then dismissed it all as somehow not quite right. As always, obsessions could serve as a blockade against whatever unpalatable external reality was going on at the time.

It was at about this time that news began to filter through in the popular press about a strange new species. It was human, male, generally wore jeans and an anorak, invariably had a beard and a grungy appearance, and made its habitat on British Rail platforms where it foraged for pointless train numbers. It didn't speak – at least not in a socially conventional sense – avoided eye contact and didn't seem to do much in the way of social interaction or sexual reproduction. During the week, when it wasn't trainspotting, it made its living crunching numbers into a computer.

Asperger's syndrome had arrived. And it had nothing to do with me – at least not as outlined above. Girls hadn't even been admitted to the Asperger Club back then; it was an exclusively male affair.

After a few months at the homeless hostel for women I found the motivation to move on. As with eating disorders, it came down to making choices: I could choose to stay there or I could choose to try at least to move on. Being alone, the choice and the effort lay with me. I chose to move on.

Lying about my situation, I secured a live-in job. It didn't last long because, as always, the boss and I hated each other, but it got me off the street. Before I left the hostel, I collected some mail that had been waiting for me at the place where I had previously worked. I learned I had won an award in a National Cosmopolitan New Journalist Competition I had entered in my previous life. I had missed the award ceremony: there are no letterboxes on the street. I bought a biography of Freud with the prize money.

On my last night at the homeless hostel I was sitting downstairs in the communal area. I had been reading my newly acquired biography and had reached that point in the reading day when my eyes were beginning to ache and the words beginning to blur. I put my head down on the table next to the book. Everyone else had presumably gone to bed. A couple of people were talking in the background: one was Deena, the Jamaican lady; the other was Elsie. They thought I was asleep and were talking about me:

'She's a sweet young girl,' Elsie said.

'She's a lovely young person. It's a shame when they end up here,' said Deena before disappearing off into the kitchen. Elsie quietly came up to me and placed a bag of crisps on the table in front of me. She smiled at me, a lovely smile, like a grandmother taking pleasure in treating a grandchild.

I looked up, stunned, afraid. Someone was offering me food, which was always a source of panic in my rigidly observed food rituals, but I was more afraid because someone was being kind to me, had said nice things about me, and I never knew what the social response to that was.

'Gaw orn,' she urged softly in her East End accent 'Eat 'em up. You look like you need a good feed.'

'Thank you,' I stammered.

It was a small incidental act of kindness from one person who had nothing to another. The memory of it, however, has stayed with me all my life. In the emotional desert I lived in, it was a drop of water, one I could accept, whereas a cupful would have overwhelmed me.

During my time in the homeless world of London I learned what kindness is – real kindness which is given freely and expects nothing back – and how this kindness is as likely, if not more likely, to come from those who have nothing. It was a lesson I have never forgotten.

In the meantime, I continued my search to find a way of dealing with the world whilst somehow trying to keep my autistic self intact. Now that I was no longer communicating with the world through the coded messages of starvation, I decided it was time I learned to talk properly, with words. I still had to keep my autistic inner world private at all costs, so I started using my brain to adapt to whoever I was with, developing a vast array of personas. I could think quickly and I learned to talk by focussing on what was said and then turning it into a question or an observation which would deflect curiosity away from myself. I often saw things in a rather offbeat way and had a habit of speaking my mind which could be either very funny or just plain rude. I could, if I wanted, make people laugh. I could think ahead of others and frequently outstrip them, and I began to use my brain to do this, to help me negotiate and survive the onslaught of daily encounters. Adopting social personas allowed me to simultaneously 'communicate' with the world and hold it at bay, keep my inner landscape free and uncontaminated whilst allowing me to explore the vast outer landscapes the world offered. But it came at a price and it was damn hard work.

And it only worked up to a point.

4

rootless

Two hundred miles inside the Norwegian Arctic Circle on the main E6 road, a blue Volvo pulled up. Traffic was sparse up here; I'd been waiting for a lift in the eerie twilight of the midnight sun for a while. It was past midnight but the birds were still singing.

'Er du norsk?' the man behind the wheel asked me.

'Nei, engelsk.'

For once I was telling the truth. Hitching alone through Europe, I regularly adopted a range of different nationalities, identities, stories, changing them to suit whoever I was with. Here, in this remote wilderness en route for the North Cape, it seemed safe enough to admit at least to being English. But that was rare in those days, when personas could change so rapidly I sometimes forgot which one I had chosen.

The man in the Volvo smiled and opened the passenger seat door. 'Good, I can practise my English then. I'm Kjell,' he said in what already sounded like perfect English.

'Thanks, I'm Karen.' I introduced someone who was not me. I fastened the seat belt and set off on one more ride into the unknown, relishing the freedom that goes with being a stranger in a strange place, encountering other strangers for brief, fixed periods.

Maybe Europe was a kinder place then. I travelled when and where I wanted freely and easily with an astounding array of people. I was young and naive enough to believe I was immortal, and the burly truck drivers of Europe, who shared with me their ferry passes, their meal expenses and their advice ('If anyone gives you any trouble, knee 'em in the balls'), were invariably kind. No one took advantage of me, though I was small, young, female and alone.

My reasoning ran that as I was already so cut off from any roots – what the French call *déraciné* – I could go anywhere and it wouldn't matter, little realising then that no one gets more homesick than those who haven't a home to go to. The urge to travel, the restless need to keep moving, keep exploring, was the same one that meant I might stay in the same house for months, bags and boxes unpacked as I remained always poised to move on, burning my bridges behind me and never stopping to watch the ensuing conflagration. It was the same urge that kept me moving from job to job, always yearning for something that was never there. I was trying to find a sense of self in the external world, but I could only interact with the external world on a fleeting, impermanent basis.

The driver of the Volvo, Kjell, pulled up and dropped me off after crossing a bridge linking the fragmented Norwegian coastline. It was starting to rain. I thanked him as he headed off to a home somewhere and I headed off to pitch my tent in a nearby cluster of trees. It was late and in the eerie twilight world I listened to the birds who would twitter all night during the months of the midnight sun and the rain pattering on the canvas. I let 'Karen', whoever she was, go and I became myself again. I breathed freely.

Travelling was part of my never-ending thirst for knowledge. With this as my principal objective, I trained to teach English as a foreign language and set off with a rucksack and a one-way bus ticket to Greece. English teachers were in big demand and I was offered the first teaching job I applied for in Athens. Prior to this, I spent a short while living in a brothel.

In my naivety I didn't know it was a brothel at the time – it was a low-grade hotel in the centre of Athens which boosted its income by its night-time trade. A nice, very old man who wandered about the dark, dingy corridors told me. 'There are bad people here,' he whispered. He told me his son was the proprietor and he was disappointed in him. He warned me not to get mixed up with the jewelled and perfumed, scantily clad ladies who seemed to mysteriously appear in the foyer every night.

Teaching didn't excite me but I got by. Confronting a room full of people was stressful and left me drained, requiring all the acting skills I'd been practising over the years. I joined a small community of expat teachers who were all slightly unconventional and accepting in the way that expats tend to be. We ate together in tavernas, drank ouzo and retsina in bars until the small hours. Weekends were spent alone, recuperating from human contact and exploring Athenian antiquity or taking the ferry from the port at Piraeus to explore the Greek islands.

I moved out of the hotel/brothel to share a flat overlooking the harbour with another teacher who had a penchant for young Greek boys and who carefully explained to me the difference between pederasty and paedophilia. Standing on the balcony watching a shoal of dolphins rising and dipping in the blue Aegean Sea in the bright white sunlight of Greece one day, I decided that for now life wasn't so bad.

But already something was stirring in me, the ever-present urge that made me break ties with people before I became overloaded by their presence, split and fragmented and feeling paralysed. It was time to move on. As winter approached, I decided to head for the sunshine of Israel and a spell on a kibbutz.

I'd been fascinated by Jewish culture and history since I'd met David and, in my obsessive way, had already studied Hebrew and Yiddish, read avidly about Zionism, the Diaspora and the Shoah, and had plans to learn Sephardi and more about the Talmud at some point. I headed off on the boat from Piraeus harbour with a third-class ticket, which entitled me to sleep on deck at the stern end. New Year arrived en route and the third-class passengers, mostly young travellers from all the continents of the earth, celebrated under the stars of the warm skies as the boat wound its way towards Haifa through the dark, island-studded Aegean Sea. Counting down to the New Year with ouzo and raki flowing freely and with that sense of shared freedom that only comes from interim periods of travel was a rare moment of inclusion. But when the boat docked on the shore at Haifa, I had a strong foreboding that it was hardly going to be a time for rejoicing.

Perhaps I had been living on borrowed time for too long. By the time I travelled from Tel Aviv to the kibbutz near the Gaza Strip, I was desperate to be alone. Unfortunately, it is hard to be alone when you share close living and working quarters with 30 other volunteers. At the kibbutz we were housed in a place call the nahal in basic huts with four bunks, overlooking a central grass courtyard. There was a shower block and a kitchen area, but meals and other facilities were mainly provided on the central kibbutz area which was a short walk away. Most of the volunteers were Europeans – Danish, Dutch and German. A few came from the Far East and South America.

Mornings began early on the kibbutz. At 5am several of us loaded into a rackety old truck which drove down dusty tracks to the pardas or orchard where the oranges were ripe for picking. We worked there in teams until after midday or until the daily quota was filled, scaling up orange trees and filling large canvas bags. Then we returned together. We also ate together, lived, breathed and slept together. Alone, I would have communed with the landscape, absorbed new sensations, smells, sights, feelings, but with others around these became blocked off, sacrificed to the sensory demands of dealing with people around me and the ensuing engulfment. I wanted everyone to go away, which, as this was supposed to be communal living, was hardly reasonable.

I felt myself become increasingly desperate. I was on edge, angry at the world. People seemed to be walking guardedly around me, sending me sideways looks. Voices in my head were telling me to kill someone and the first person in line was me. Something was going horribly wrong.

I didn't tell anyone about the man I had met in the streets in Tel Aviv before joining the kibbutz, the man who had invited me up to his apartment for a coffee, and how, in my autistic naivety, 'come up for coffee' had meant just that. On the kibbutz I could still feel him, forcing me on to the floor of his apartment, one hand holding me down whilst the other forced open the zip of my jeans. 'Just relax,' he said, ramming his hand against my jaw. It was the same advice Tim had given me several years previously. I froze and went still, staring up at the light bulb on the ceiling. I was no longer inside myself; I had split off into someone else again.

Afterwards he offered me the coffee I had come for.

I didn't link what had happened in Tel Aviv with what was happening now. The brutal physical violation merged with a wider sense that my inner self was being violated by too much human contact. I couldn't process things any more, couldn't put my finger on what was happening to me. But one thing was becoming apparent: I needed to be alone, to recover back the self which I felt had been split for too long and into too many fragments in the external world. When each new encounter requires a new persona, a new adaptation, it becomes exhausting. Teaching had stretched me to the limit and now, living in a communal situation, I was approaching breaking point. Something had to give.

Increasingly I withdrew from everyone at every opportunity, disappearing into the woods near the nahal where I concocted wild escape plans of moving on to India or going to China. In fact, I didn't have the money to do either, and on some level I knew that I needed to stop running away and to retreat back into myself if I was going to have any hope of piecing my severely fragmented self back together. The only possibility appeared to be to return to England, but I did not seem able to make any rational decisions. And then events overtook me.

The volunteers returning from a party on the main part of the kibbutz were drunk. I could hear them shouting and fumbling in the dark from where I lay on my bunk, cold, my teeth starting to chatter. They staggered into the hut noisily and the light switch flicked on.

'*Fucking hell, what's happened here?*'

'*You spilt some wine, Sue?*'

'*Aww, shit, that's the last red we had.*'

'*That's not wine.*'

Someone was still mopping up blood when the ambulance took me to the hospital.

Alone in my empty hut in the nahal, I had picked up a nail that I had earmarked earlier as a potential implement. The first superficial scratches weren't satisfactory – a necklace of blood beads on the surface of my white arm. This was going to have to be a big one to shift the monstrous thing that was inside me now. An empty brown beer bottle stood on the floor. I smashed it on the stone steps outside my hut, revealing two glinting jagged edges. I drew one edge tentatively across the white skin. I could feel my heart starting to pound. When it came, the final cut split the flesh, revealing a red, raw wound which gaped inches wide like an open mouth for a brief second before blood such as I had never seen before welled up and surged out.

Shit!

Blood was pooling all down me, all over the floor. In a moment of panic which left no time for thought, it came to me in a flash – a life-saving memory from a first-aid course I'd done some time ago: *Cover it fast and keep covering it.* The bed sheet wound round and round and still the blood kept coming through. I was feeling dizzy. I curled up on the bed, and with the sheet wound around my arm, held it tight above my head. I lay there and waited to see what would happen.

The nurses and doctor who saw me were clearly not happy that I was wasting their time with a self-injury. The other scars on my arm were too much of a giveaway for me to pretend it was anything other than that.

I had self-harmed before – often it felt like the only resource available to me to deal with negative feelings in my isolated world, or to force myself to feel something when I became too numb or cut off. Strangely, it always seemed to make things temporarily better, replacing one kind of hurt with another which was visible and tangible and more real, and which would go away soon anyway. It was a coping mechanism, not a suicide bid, and as long as I remembered to wear long sleeves at work it wasn't really a problem; I remained detached from the scars that were filling up the space on my arms.

'Don't do it again,' the doctor told me severely when they had finished stitching me up. At that point I had no intention and I could see his point. People living in what was effectively a war zone have better things to do, and I really had not wanted to bring myself to anyone else's attention. But at the same time I hadn't known what else to do or who to turn to, and, for better or for worse, the self-harm had done its work. I felt a huge burden had lifted from me, spilled out like the blood I had lost. I was calm, almost happy.

No one else was.

When I returned to the kibbutz, the other volunteers, who had previously regarded me as weird, were now avoiding me even more. I sat alone at the lunch table, spoke to no one and, as I was taken off work duties, mooched around more or less alone at the nahal all day. When I emerged from the hut, heads went down, looked away. People were hushed around me. It felt awkward and horrible: I didn't want to be a social pariah; I just wanted to be out of society. One moment of redemption came when, as I was sitting apart from everyone else with my back against a tree, a lovely young Dutch girl detached herself from a group of friends and came up to me.

'I thought you might like this, Susan.'

She showed me a poem she'd liked about a traveller who felt he was no longer able to travel because he felt himself becoming attached to the people and places he visited, and every parting had become a wrench. It was a mirror image of my own situation. I wanted to move on, move away, achieve perfect detachment.

The kibbutz authorities were kind to me but took a dim view of what had happened. Thinking that I must have been suicidal (in fact, I hadn't been), they presented me with a choice: psychiatric hospital in Jerusalem or return home. By mutual agreement, I bought a plane ticket home. I wanted to go back to Britain where everything was familiar anyway; I missed the grey, rainy skies, decent tea, warm beer. I also wanted a room of my own, somewhere to retreat to lick my wounds. The kibbutz didn't mean anything unkindly; they were worried about me and just thought I'd be better off with family and friends in my own home. I didn't bother to explain that there was no one there I wanted or felt able to go to.

A few days before I left to come back to Britain, I wandered into the small wooded area near the nahal. I'd go there often to get away from the other volunteers and would sit on the sandy semi-desert ground under the trees. Usually I brought my Hebrew dictionary to learn some vocabulary or a book I'd borrowed from the kibbutz library. This time I came empty-handed. I couldn't read any more – I was still shell-shocked and anaemic after the previous episode. I lay on the sandy floor and looked at the trees and the plant life that survives in arid conditions. I was looking at it through a silver haze. Slowly the tear dropped out of my eye and ran down my cheek. In my clearer vision I saw a wild tortoise making its painfully slow way across the clearing.

I had always liked tortoises – I remembered my childhood pet, Hifi, with affection. In the woods I watched the wild tortoise as I had watched Hifi walk across the garden lawn as a carefree child, but now there was a sadness inside me that felt like an ancient weariness, as ancient as the species itself, years of aching aloneness that would never end, as if God himself had cut me off.

The tortoise stopped to nibble at a leaf, its ancient, scaly head, which had survived like this probably since the dawn of evolution, stretching upwards on its ancient, scraggy neck. Its completeness struck me in my shattered, fragmented place. I envied its primordial survival methods, its freedom to live wholly and exclusively within itself, the home it carried everywhere on its back. How and why along the evolutionary thrust had we allowed it all to become so complicated and exhausting, so difficult that just lying down and going to sleep forever here and now seemed preferable?

The tears were dropping down my face. I wasn't sobbing – I rarely cried, being mostly unable to access all but the more simple emotions – but something was stirring inside me, a realisation that I now had no choice but to face the limitations of myself that I had come up against. By running round the world, I had been playing the hare to the tortoise – literally haring around. But what was I running to and would I ever get there? And if I got there, wouldn't I have to run even further, even faster, in some elusive search to belong in an alien society? I had passed my twenties with a vague but unspecified conviction that one day I would graduate into that normality of relationships and security and connectedness to a time and place in the world going on outside me. By travelling, I had tried to have some share of it, and as long as I was on the move and unattached I seemed to cope, but it was when I stopped that I always seemed to crash against the invisible glass wall of the social world. And in this final crashing realisation that normality, the everyday world that I could see but not touch, was always going to be beyond my reach, a question came to me. Like all earth-shattering questions, it was deceptively simple: *Do you really want to be a part of it?*

And the answer came back from inside, clear and instant: *No!*

Being with others did not make me happy. Being alone did not in itself make me unhappy. The painful, aching desolation of aloneness that had characterised my younger adult years and all the years before had mutated into an acceptance that social relationships were just not for me. It was a final realisation that I didn't have to *try* to belong any more because I *couldn't*. My best option seemed to lie in developing the inner world, focussing on finding a place there. This was, after all, the world I would carry with me wherever I went – much like a tortoise carapace. That moment in the woods in Israel was the beginning of a breakthrough, a moment when, in the words of the hymn, all our strivings cease, a surrender to what *is* rather than a battle to gain what can never be. I didn't know *what* was wrong, but I could accept that *something* was wrong and that in all likelihood it would never be right: I was never going to fit in, never going to be a part of a wider external world. And the myriad of separate personas I had created, those false social selves that enabled me to interact with others whilst giving away nothing of myself because they were not me, the ones that kept me endlessly on the run and rootless, were no longer needed. To maintain a sense of integrity, to survive whole and intact, nature had ordained that I keep myself apart. It was time to make peace with what was.

My time in Israel produced a breakdown but also a breakthrough. I was wiser but not sadder afterwards. Self-acceptance came slowly, not always helped by the endless battering of social pressures which object to us for daring to be different, for being resolutely single in a world made for two, for refusing to accept that we should be happy and socialise at Christmas, celebrate our birthdays with a party, have children, form families, be normal... No matter. All social pressures of the above kind would eventually be met in me with one resounding *Who says so?* And yes, who does say so? Only the imaginary notions of a society to which I was no longer trying to belong.

So I arrived in my thirties, not as most of my contemporaries probably did, worrying about the ticking of the biological clock, building up careers and families, and consolidating mortgages and material possessions. For the first time I was learning to live inside myself whilst still being around others and fully accepting the cut-off person I was.

In years to come I would learn that being inside yourself around others can be the most dangerous place of all.

5

a dog called minder

It was shortly after I'd returned from Israel that a dog called Minder came into my life. Unable to get a mortgage and facing the high costs of renting in Oxford, I was living alone on a houseboat on the far reaches of the Thames at the time. It was an isolated but fairly bohemian lifestyle and, if you didn't pay too much attention to what occasionally floated past your porthole, quite a pleasant one.

One day I was returning down the towpath to my boat with wood for the stove when I stopped in my tracks. A very large white dog with black spots and a patch over his eye was lying on the grass, licking his paws. I've always had some sort of radar for animals, honing in on them in a way that is diametrically opposed to the way I tend to close down around people. This dog seemed to sense it because as I approached he stood up, wagging his long white tail and making that most characteristic of Dalmatian gestures – the smile. Dalmatians have always been my favourite dog, and whilst this one wasn't a pure-bred pedigree, he had enough characteristics of the breed to make me gasp.

'Hey, fella!' The sound of my own voice surprised me – it had been so long since I had spoken voluntarily or initiated a conversation. I probably smiled back at him too – that was also a strange thing to do. He wagged his tail even more and started to wiggle his back end, then, still smiling, he pushed his face against my leg. I dropped the wood and went down on my knees. Then I did something that was even stranger: my hands reached out towards him to scratch behind his ears. I was anything but tactile as a rule. I needed a lot of space around me, a kind of exclusion zone which could be alternately a fortress to keep the world out or a prison to keep me in. Naturally bypassing all this, this big soppy dog pushed his head against me for more and more scratching.

'You'd better come in,' I said at last. On the boat we shared some biscuits and it gave me a curious sense of pleasure to watch him eat in my unnurtured and unnurturing world. Eventually, and reluctantly, I decided it was time to let him go back to wherever he lived. Minder (for so his name read on the tag on his collar) seemed in no hurry to go; in fact, eventually I had to lead him off the boat by his collar and close the door.

Next day I woke to a strange noise – a high-pitched squeaking sound. At first I thought it was something mechanical and my heart sank: I was no good at fixing things and I never had anyone to do it for me. I followed the sound which was actually coming from beyond the cabin door. Sitting outside was Minder, his head raised to the sky, emitting a series of squeaks which stopped midway as he saw me and bounded inside. I appeared to have made a friend.

He came round regularly after that, sharing my meals, sharing the space and the silence. I looked forward to his visits and, as they became more and more frequent, I bought him his own bowls to eat and drink from, included dog food on the shopping list which had erstwhile only been for one, and brushed his fur far more than I ever brushed my own hair. He adopted, as dogs will, the best place in front of the fire as his to lie on, and he began to stay overnight, insisting on curling up on the end of the bed. He woke me up in the morning by pushing his wet nose against my face and whining softly until I gave him the attention he craved. I began to miss him when he wasn't there.

But his visits left me wondering why no one came looking for him. His name tag had no address but I had seen him once or twice on a nearby campsite which was part of some kind of Thames country club. Overcoming my normal reticence, I spoke to several caravan owners and learned that whilst Minder belonged in name to the campsite no one seemed to have direct ownership of him. Nominally he was a guard dog but that really was in name only – one affectionate pat and Minder was anybody's, a treat and he was yours for life, or at least till the next one came along.

'It's not fair on him,' one of the caravan owners said. 'He's a fantastic dog and he deserves a good home.' It seemed that Minder got by visiting various caravanners. He was a great favourite with many of them, but in dog terms it was less than satisfactory, dogs preferring to have one owner, a pack leader they can rely on and live with as part of a pack for life. It made sense in the way he had attached to me: Minder was looking for an owner. Once again, motivated by an animal far more than I ever was by a human, I decided to overcome my natural reserve and ask at the club if I could take him on. The manager, who was slowly getting drunk in the bar, eyed me lecherously and said,

'Take him if you want him. This place is going under so he'll be homeless soon.' So Minder came to live in my autistic world.

He was larger than life in every sense and inclined to porkiness due to having been neutered (not helped by his seemingly endless capacity for extracting treats from people). The large black patch over one eye gave him a rakish piratical appearance which went well with living on my boat. I sometimes speculated about his parentage: some Dalmatian certainly, but something else rather large and bulkier. Maybe there was some Labrador in him – he certainly ate like one. But everyone who met him agreed on one thing: somehow a bit of human had sneaked into his genetic makeup. Minder was the most intelligent, perceptive dog I had ever met and, like many rescue dogs who have been passed around from owner to owner, he was extremely loyal when he did find someone he could call his own. When he knew that he was going to stay with me, his love and gratitude were boundless.

On the surface we were opposites. I was withdrawn, silent and expected little. Minder was sociable, an inveterate communicator in his dog-like way and, despite the ups and downs of his life, seemed endlessly optimistic. To me, the world was a confusing, complex place, both socially and emotionally, whereas Minder seemed to have effortlessly solved the meaning of life and found the path to serenity: food, company, warmth and exercise made you happy, and once these were satisfied there was nothing else to do but sleep peacefully through the day until the next meal came along.

For all that we were opposites, however, we seemed to have formed a remarkable bond. He stayed with me physically but also entered my mental space which worked desperately hard to keep everyone else out in the interests of self-preservation.

With Minder, something very strange started to happen: I wanted him to be around all the time. He was never invasive, he didn't talk beyond the basics of requesting to be let out or fed, he demanded nothing of me, he accepted me in all my autistic eccentricity, he was easy to read, having only simple emotions, and his attitude to life was inspiring. Normally, after any time spent in the presence of another person, I wanted to be alone. I could be with Minder all day and still keep all the advantages of being alone.

Now when I woke up I had someone else to think about, someone to look after, someone who would look after me – my very own minder. In a paradoxical way a dog was effectively making me more like a human and, in my eyes, Minder seemed to become more human every day. With Minder, I talked, the nonsense all dog owners talk to their dogs. I never minded his interruptions into the hitherto sacrosanct space of my private thoughts, and I began to think in terms of the two of us. The autistic 'I' had become 'We'.

Of course, it could have been just me seeing what I wanted to see and believing what I wanted to believe, but Minder proved to me once and for all that animals have a capacity to reach out to the most cut-off people that is remarkable.

At the time I was barely able to hold down a job, but I had secured a badly paid, part-time post working nights in a hostel for homeless men. The hostel was fairly old-style, seemingly working on the principle that putting a lot of damaged people together under one roof with minimal staff was economically viable if nothing else. The men at the hostel were homeless for varying reasons – alcohol was a prevalent cause on the surface, but beneath that often lay a tragic story of abuse, children's homes, ex-soldiers back from various war zones with undiagnosed post-traumatic stress disorder. One or two older ones were veterans of the Second World War who had never really readjusted to civilian life; one man had lost his home during the London Blitz and had been homeless ever since. A few of the men were gays who had grown up forced to live unhappy closet lives in intolerant times. Quite a large number of the residents had mental illnesses and, with the closing down of the large psychiatric institutions, had ended up in the hostel, unable to cope on the outside, many repeatedly going through the revolving door of acute psychiatric wards to care in the community to acute psychiatric wards *ad nauseam*. Others had learning difficulties or physical disabilities or were just too vulnerable to cope. The reasons for the men being there were as many as the individuals themselves, but all were damaged and vulnerable and could often hide this behind alcohol and violent, aggressive behaviour. Although, in many ways, I was worlds apart from these men, I always felt fairly at home amongst them. Again, the radar that links life's outsiders seemed to be operating. But one thing always struck me: the vast majority were more socially needy than me.

Now that I had Minder, I worried about leaving him alone when I was away at work overnight. Doubtless he would happily have slept through on the boat and woken overjoyed (a) to see me and (b) to be fed in the morning, but I was a new owner and I felt my responsibility for him. I decided to take him with me. I worked alone with one caretaker and sneaked Minder in after the other staff had gone for the night. I wasn't sure how the residents would react, and my intention was to keep him in the office overnight where he could sleep and then sneak him out to the car the next morning. But first I decided to let him introduce himself.

When Minder trotted into the communal area on his first night, a transformation took place. People who were slumped in indifference or doped up on medications suddenly sat up and took notice. Lots of people clicked to him or whistled and called out to him. One man – let's call him Bob – who had existed in his own peculiar schizophrenic world for many years, who never communicated other than to ask for a cigarette or to get his basic needs met, left off endlessly pacing the room, smiled and went over to greet him.

Within a few seconds, more people were smiling and talking to each other than I had ever witnessed there before.

'What's his name?' asked Gordon, who had a mental age of six, and volunteered to walk him in the morning.

'Steady now – good boy!' Colin, who had been busy snatching at imaginary radio wires sending him special messages when we walked in, had started teaching Minder to balance a biscuit on his nose. Minder took it all very calmly in his stride, working his way round the room to be patted and fed treats in exchange for a lick or a shake of a paw. It didn't matter to Minder that these were amongst society's most marginalised: they were friendly, they wanted to know him and he responded in kind with no judgement or questions or worry about what anyone would think. Strange behaviour or appearance wasn't a problem in his dog's perception of things – he could sense that no one meant him any harm. I watched from the doorway, astonished. So it hadn't been just me that Minder was able to get through to. This was several years before much in the way of research had been done on the therapeutic effects of animals in a residential setting, but any proof needed was there in front of me that night.

I took Minder every night after that and each night I watched him work his transformation in those lost and broken worlds. It became the highlight of people's day, many of them saving up treats for him from their meals. It didn't help Minder's waistline, but it gave people a sense of something to care about, something to look after in a world where this must have often seemed remote. Inevitably, the manager found out but he took the view that anything that improved the quality of people's lives in whatever way was a good thing. It became axiomatic that Minder did more good that the rest of the staff put together, and he became an honorary team member, the one everyone loved. Ever after when I saw the effect of animals on people in this way, I mentally dubbed it 'the Minder Effect'.

I didn't know then that one day I was going to benefit personally from this effect more than I could have ever imagined.

Part 2

A World Turned
Upside Down

6

first encounters

A few years on into the new millennium I had moved a long way from the chaos and confusion that had hallmarked my early adult years as someone with an autism spectrum disorder trying to function in a neurotypical world. Although it would be a few more years before I was officially diagnosed with Asperger's/autism and, as for many females, diagnosis came relatively late, I knew that I was and always would be fundamentally different in my relationship with the world around me. I had learned to respect the needs of my autistic world whilst trying to balance them against the demands of the outer world. It was still a struggle, but I seemed to have worked out an uneasy compromise. Because I had reached a measure of self-acceptance, recognising what I could and could not do in terms of relating to the world, I found it easier to get along in social situations, no longer feeling that I had to become a different person with everyone I met. I had developed some of the social skills that others take for granted, and I found that I could get on with people for brief periods at least and that moreover they often quite liked my quirky independence.

I had moved on in other ways too, training as a journalist and working as a freelance writer and travel researcher. Whilst the solitary, focussed work suited me, making enough money to live on was always an issue in my resolutely single world, and I still had to spend more time holding down temporary and part-time jobs in the outer world than I would have liked. But overall the chaos and confusion of my earlier years were receding. As the new millennium dawned, time seemed ripe for external changes, bringing me to a new place to live and work. I moved up north to Yorkshire from the south of England, but although it was a new beginning, I didn't expect the world inside my autistic bubble to change. It was fundamentally static, a closed system, no matter how much things changed on the outside; I remained isolated, cut off, and struggled whenever I had to deal with the world around me. And in all probability nothing would have changed on the inside had it not been for an extraordinary chain of events.

Not long into the new century I applied for a job as a night worker at a probation hostel, supervising offenders living in the community. After the interview I received a phone call at home telling me I had been successful. The man at the other end of the phone paused. I could feel some hesitation in his voice: 'I need to ask you, though, are you really sure you want the job? We have to offer it to you because you were so much better than the other candidates, but we all thought you were too intelligent for it. You'll be spending a lot of quiet time on your own there at night.'

It was a familiar story. In order to preserve my autistic world from the overload of the everyday world, I frequently had to opt for work that would demand little of me, where for the most part I could be alone, preferably where I would have time to read to fuel my voracious inner life and the space to write. Although I had a number of post-graduate qualifications, I was on a permanently low income in jobs that didn't really use much skill and where I was always operating well below my actual abilities. This rankled sometimes, but always it came down to a case of survive on a pittance with self intact or aim for something higher and risk annihilation. There really wasn't much choice.

The deal with the new job was that I would work with another worker from 10pm until midnight, be on my own till 7am and have two hours in the morning still to work with someone else. So that meant potentially seven hours alone. I had long ago realised that in the interests of autistic self-preservation I needed a ratio of time alone that exceeded the time I spent with others. I hadn't quite got it down to a mathematical formula, but a ratio of four hours in company to seven hours alone didn't sound too far off, if erring a little too much on the company side. It was the kind of calculation I had to make on a daily basis and was one of a myriad of small stresses that added up to the daily battle of getting through the day.

'Yes, I want it,' I said. I needed a proper job – I had just bought my first house. I little knew then what a fateful decision I was making.

'In that case, congratulations and welcome on board, and I'd urge you to seek promotion whenever the opportunity comes up.'

I cringed slightly at the words 'welcome on board', with their implication that I was going to be expected to be part of something. Already my mind had started calculating how long I would stay there.

Whilst it might seem strange that I had opted to work with people, this effectively served two purposes. Because my private world was so shut off and isolated, I needed some contact, which I could not get from working at a computer all day. Effectively, working with others meant that I would not drift too far out into complete isolation, which I knew from experience was debilitating and could lead to an eventual deadening inside. The other purpose was that in a work environment there were built-in barriers and boundaries between me and those I worked with. It was much safer than the freewheeling world of private personal relationships.

So although the new job didn't look set to be too challenging, it accommodated to some extent my autistic self. What I called my self-preservation racket would, as far as I knew at the time, still be intact.

The probation hostel where I began to work was host to five convicted murderers, eight serial child sex offenders, a pending case of child murder, a couple of rapists and several violent assault cases. The prisons were in their usual crisis of overcrowding and there was yet another government initiative to treat criminals in the community wherever possible, with the consequence that more serious offenders were likely to stay in the community and those serving prison sentences for very serious crimes were more likely to get parole than at previous times.

The hostel was set in a semi-genteel residential area whose inhabitants mowed their lawns on Sunday and went off to respectable jobs on Monday oblivious of who lived in their midst. The building was, or had been, a large, wealthy residence, perhaps that of a former mill owner who had moved on to the more respectable suburbs of Ilkley or Otley or had perhaps reached that ultimate destination of social respectability in Yorkshire – Harrogate. It stood in its own grounds and each resident had their own room; there was a dining room for communal activities, a kitchen, various offices and a sleep-in room for staff. The hostel was staffed around the clock every day of the year, with workers reducing to two for the night shift, only one of whom (me) would be awake and available to deal with residents.

On the whole the staff were excellent – dedicated, fair, determined to try to work with people whatever the crime or history of crime. There was a wide range of ages and backgrounds, and nearly everyone got on – working together at unsocial hours around the clock breeds its own sense of community. In spite of my usual misgivings about being able to fit in anywhere, I found myself accepted and for the most part it was a place where I felt reasonably happy to work, if work I must. Despite or maybe because of the stresses of the job, we spent a lot of time laughing and joking.

The world of the hostel was closed and tightknit. Residents were there under strict supervision, bound by curfews and restricted in their movements within the community. Any breach of these conditions and they could be called straight back to prison. For sex offenders in particular (the majority of the residents), prison could be a place of intense harassment. In the prison hierarchy, sex offenders, especially those who committed crimes against children, were the lowest of the low and tales were legion of glass being sneaked into their food, beatings and endless harassment, even though most opted for segregation within the prison. To avoid going back there, the vast majority, on the surface at least, were highly compliant.

In many ways I liked and got on well with the majority of the residents. If you didn't think too hard about what they had done – and on the whole it was better not to – most of them were quite pleasant. Having sinned against society, they were society's outcasts, undesirable and untouchable by any good, upstanding citizen. With low self-esteem and limited prospects, most were quite anxious to prove that they weren't all bad. And none of them was *all* bad. As always, the unconscious radar that links life's outsiders worked for me; I seemed better able to relate to them than to so-called 'normal' people. With autism, where each and every encounter in the world can potentially be like walking into a room full of tarantulas, where unwanted eye contact and a smile or an arbitrary piece of kindness can seem so threatening, a few hardened criminals was neither more nor less scary, in the way that spending a session alone in a room with someone can seem scarier than standing on a platform facing a thousand faces.

There was quite a bit of movement amongst the hostel resident population. Sometimes the hostel was a short stopgap place for men to stay between release from prison and moving on to more settled accommodation; sometimes an inability to keep the 11pm curfew meant residents were recalled to prison. Breach of rules, absconding and prison sentencing could all lead to removal. A few residents whom I got to know quite well were under a court order to reside at the hostel for a longer period as an alternative to custody.

One day we were expecting a new resident. He had been released early from prison on condition that he resided at the hostel and participated in a number of prescribed community programmes. M – let's call him that (to this day I cannot say his first name and his surname was that of a well-known brand of food which to this day also I cannot bring myself to buy) – came with an unappealing record. He was a serial mugger of vulnerable people, mainly the elderly, described as having been in the criminal system for most of his adult life (he was now in his thirties) and with no fear of prison. His report did not make good reading. The mugshot was equally unendearing: shaven head, scarred, acne-pocked face, tattooed and with a prison pallor. But what was most disturbing were the eyes: lifeless, cold blue eyes with pupils like pinpricks.

'Looks like Freddie,' a male colleague commented.

'Who's Freddie?'

'Kruger. Freddie Kruger – *Nightmare on Elm Street*.'

We were all well-schooled in not judging people on the basis of their appearance but had to concede that this particular face was stretching us a little.

I met him a few days later. In the flesh there wasn't much improvement. He was medium height but powerful and well built. Time spent in the prison gym had probably played a part in that. Prisoners with time on their hands often worked out; if they didn't get caught up in the illicit drug culture rife in some of the prisons, they could leave very fit, with more energy than they knew what to do with. I came across him in the corridor outside his room and recognised him immediately from the photo. I introduced myself and asked when he had arrived. Brushing aside my question, he asked, 'Where are you from?'

He spoke with a curiously soft, almost gentle, Geordie accent which contrasted eerily with his appearance.

I was taken aback by his question. It was overfamiliar and, besides, I never invited personal questions from anyone. To avoid being asked, I would sometimes go on the offensive and bombard people with them, having worked out that most people's favourite topic of conversation is themselves. It was a defence technique, but it worked for me and was fairly socially acceptable.

'Quite a way off,' I said.

'Come in here for a minute.' He invited me into his room, again in that strange, soft voice. When I hesitated, he added, 'I'll show you what I've made.'

There were no rules about going in residents' rooms or being alone with them in a confined space. The ethos of the hostel was to break down barriers, to treat people as normal wherever possible. At the time I didn't question it. I stepped into his room.

'Look.' On his drawer was a traditional gypsy caravan made from matchsticks, a favourite recreational activity of the long-term incarcerated. It was impressive and represented hours of painstaking work. I admired it.

'How long did it take to make?' I asked, genuinely curious. Again, he ignored my question.

'Look at this.' He picked up the caravan and opened the minute front door. Inside, a tiny electric light bulb lit up. Whilst I was looking at it, I sensed his eyes focussing on me, boring into me. Suddenly he touched my hair.

'Your hair's nice,' he said.

A warning frisson went through me. I turned and met the cold, hard eyes. 'Don't do that, please.' I handed the caravan back to him and left.

Back in the office, I felt strange. He had overstepped the usual boundaries but seemed to have had no awareness that he had done anything wrong. Boundaries between staff and residents were mostly implicit, mostly fully understood on both sides without the need to spell it out. It was not something I ever had an issue with anyway. My autistic personality had a boundary wound round it so tightly that I am told it is almost palpable. On a personal and a professional level, I was inviting nobody in. And yet now my instincts were sounding a warning bell, low-level but there.

Everyone else was busy so I did not mention what had happened, and by the time I left to go home I had rationalised it to myself: he was just fresh out of the sex-starved world of prison, I was probably one of the first females he had come into contact with, he was not yet fully adjusted to being on the outside.

I drove home across the moors, looking forward to seeing the dogs. I had had several dogs since Minder, none of them quite so well behaved. I was met by the full-on greeting that only two boisterous Dalmatians can give. Poppy, the older one, a liver-spotted Dal, was settling a little – in fact, for a Dalmatian she was to become quite a sedate dog. Dessie was black-spotted and, at less than a year old, had yet to have any inkling of what restraint meant. She licked me to within an inch of my life and the outside world began to recede as the inner autistic one was allowed out again.

I shared this world only with the dogs and it was difficult for me to leave them. Bending down to pat them, I promised them that one day we'd have more time to spend together. Little did I know how soon that was going to be.

7

assault

I usually worked off the stresses of the outside world by walking the dogs. Here in Yorkshire, close to the heart of Brontë country, I could pound across the moors getting a taste of the *Wuthering Heights*-type landscape every day. The vast open moors still thrilled me after the overcrowded city life of Oxford. Often, if you climbed high enough on the hills, you could find that rare luxury of 360 degrees of all-round vision; space opened up around you everywhere you looked, the moorland populated only by distant herds of scraggy sheep. The 'silence' was such that every sound could be heard – the rush of the wind, the cry of the curlews, the bleating of the distant sheep in an astonishing range of registers echoing across the valleys. It fitted perfectly with my autistic self, providing a purifying journey that washed away the outside world. If I saw someone else out walking (which was rare), it disturbed the process, breached the strict demarcation between time inside and time outside, sent my anxiety levels soaring. In those days even a distant figure on the horizon could do this, causing me to turn back or walk a different way to avoid them.

By the time I returned to work at the hostel two days later on Friday night, I was once again freed from the outside world and I had all but forgotten M.

At the start of each shift we had a handover period, a chance to update incoming staff with what had been happening and to raise any concerns there might be over the residents. M appeared to have settled in up to a point, but he had expressed some anger at having to be at the hostel now that he was no longer in prison, failing or refusing to grasp that early release had brought certain conditions with it – namely to reside at the hostel and abide by a set of parole conditions. It wasn't uncommon for ex-prisoners to show resentment at this, and staff could sometimes become the butt of this resentment, being perceived as substitute gaolers and a hindrance to freedom. The upshot was that M was described as 'a bit dodgy', a verdict rapidly subsumed by the need to monitor other violent, criminal and disturbed men who were deemed to be more of a risk to the outside community.

I didn't see much of M that night. He had been celebrating his early release at the local pub and only returned a few minutes before the 11 o'clock curfew. He was slightly the worse for wear and very full of a conquest he claimed to have made with the barmaid. My female work colleague and I avoided exchanging glances as he sat in the office telling us about his infallible chat-up line, about how the girl was dying to meet him again.

'I bet she's begging for it,' he leered. I looked at his shaven head, his pockmarked skin, the cold blue eyes, and listened to that soft, sinister voice. Something was giving me the creeps, over and beyond what I was seeing and hearing. It wasn't a feeling I had very often, but the contrast between his self-styled super-stud image and the present reality suggested something more seriously amiss. My colleague sent him on his way.

Later, when she had gone to bed, he stopped me on the corridor outside his room as I was doing a late-night check on rooms to see that no one had broken the curfew (fire escapes were the preferred exit route). It started with some general, slightly rambling small talk, including a few more references to his earlier 'conquest'. It rapidly became personal and overfamiliar, as he asked again where I lived.

'Have you got a boyfriend?'

'Yes,' I lied. In fact, I hadn't been in a relationship for some time. I'd accepted that every time a new man came into my life it would be great for a week or so and then I'd be climbing the walls, longing for my own space again, desperate to make my own choices, feeling paralysed and trapped. It was easier not to go down that route in the first place and I had by now relegated intimate relationships to the 'Been there, done that' section of the bucket list. But in places like this it was a permissible lie. Some single female members of staff were known to wear wedding rings to deter such questions.

'You could have another one, though,' he persisted, a nasty leer flashing across his cold, fish-like eyes.

'I don't need another one,' I told him, making it very clear that this conversation was at an end.

Later in the office I took the (for me) unprecedented step of flagging up a warning to other staff to make sure appropriate boundaries were kept with this resident. The warning bells at the back of my mind had just gone up a few more decibels.

The following evening things got worse. Not only was M in and out of the office, sitting on and behind the desk until told to move, but he was still regaling us with details of his supposed conquest of the night before. The details became increasingly salacious and inappropriate. We asked him to leave the office. He did so, clearly not happy.

One of my jobs was to check if any residents needed an early call in the morning; a few had secured jobs or needed to do work in the community as part of their probation order. I duly asked everyone, pausing to have a chat and catch up with those I had not seen earlier. I normally enjoyed doing this: there was usually a lot of banter about and I enjoyed the self-deprecating male humour, finding it easier to deal with than more nuanced talk about emotions or shared confidences. But tonight there was one part I did not enjoy. M, sensing an audience, proceeded to ask for an early-morning call from me with some requests that were definitely not in the job description. I felt things had gone far enough. It was the weekend and we were on limited staff (two female workers to 20 high-risk male offenders, to be precise). There would be no managers available till Monday. I did not want this to continue, especially as I would be working alone for the next seven hours.

I called him into the office and put it to him very clearly that his behaviour was unacceptable. He claimed not to know what I was talking about. I cited some examples of his inappropriate behaviour back to him. Whether he recognised that he had done something wrong or not, I don't know, but at least he acknowledged what I was saying and, looking sheepish, held up his hands:

'Yeah, I know, I'm sorry. I didn't mean to offend anyone.'

He left on a promise not to repeat that kind of behaviour again. I felt relieved; perhaps this had finally got through to him. I hoped to finish the rest of the shift without incident and started getting ready for my colleague to go off to the sleep-in room.

When the attack came, I was sitting with my back to the office door. At first I thought it was a joke, a rather creepy one in which a resident had crept up behind me and jokingly put his hands around my neck. The fingers around my neck felt curiously gentle, almost caressing at first, and then I felt something else – something cold and hard. A soft human voice, so soft it was almost playful, murmured in my ear, 'I'm going to kill you.' I felt my body go suddenly weak and powerless. I heard my work colleague shouting from behind the desk, 'No, no! Get off her!'

I twisted round to my feet and saw him standing in front of me with a kitchen knife. 'I'm going to kill you,' he said again, quietly, matter-of-fact.

He lunged towards me with the knife. I raised my arms in instinctive self-defence as he began punching at me, the rock hard blows of a man who has worked in a prison gym for years. He sent me to the floor, where I covered my head to ward off the hammering blows. Somewhere above, through my arms, I could see my colleague bravely trying to tackle him and I heard him shouting, 'Right, you're going to get it now!'

He pushed her over towards the desk. Behind the desk was a panic button, a direct link to the nearest police station. I rose to my feet, hearing her desperately calling for help, her desperate voice going out to somewhere in the universe, a million miles from where we were in the room.

I grabbed his arm as he punched her, swinging my full body weight on it. It barely had any impact on its power. The thought flashed through my mind as I looked into his demented face, contorted with fury: maybe this is what they mean when someone has demonic strength. 'I'm going to kill you, you fucking bitch,' he said. I looked into his eyes, his cold, lifeless eyes, and knew he meant it.

I don't know how many times he punched me with the knife as he held me against the wall with one hand. A realisation flashed through my head: *This is it. I'm going to die.* Followed by a long, searing internal plea to the universe: *Not yet. It's too early. I'm not ready to go yet!* Regret for the unlived life I was sure I was losing flooded me as I went outside of myself. I distinctly remember feeling as if I had moved out of my body to the left and was watching a demented beating taking place on my own body. The body fell to the floor, first to its knees and then into a foetal curl, the head grasped between the hands, waiting for the skull, which was being repeatedly slammed back against the wall, to break. There were no more pleas to the universe. I knew it was over and, as I watched myself, the only thought was a resigned one: *I hope this is quick. I hope I lose consciousness soon.* How many blows, I wondered, before a skull breaks, before the soft thudding cracks it open like an egg?

And then a miracle happened. The beating stopped. I looked up at him through a gap in my arms. He was standing over me and we made eye contact for the last time. This time his eyes registered mine. Maybe he saw the pleading in my eyes; maybe it was the greatest of ironies that I who struggled so much to make eye contact in the everyday world saved my life by doing it. Maybe he knew the alarm bell would lead to help coming. Anyway, he stopped.

He stepped back from me. 'I'll kill you,' he said softly. But it was different – a future tense, not now, later, one day…

He turned and ran from the office, through the emergency exit door released by the alarm bell, and disappeared into the night.

It was over. Perhaps a few minutes had passed or a few seconds, but it had felt like forever, and in that miniscule portion of time my life was irrevocably changed. How often our lives can change within a few seconds – a near-death experience on the operating table, a car crash that looks set to be fateful, a man yielding a knife…

What followed after is something of a blur. My work colleague, who had been so brave in trying to help me, was shaking and crying.

'Are you all right?'

'Yes.' In the immediate aftermath there was no pain, just the hyper-alertness of adrenalin pumping round in wave after wave. We hugged. We had survived.

A crowd of residents peered curiously into the office. No one had been around to witness the attack, a rarity in that setting, and ironic because I have no doubt at all that they would have done everything they could to protect us. A barrage of questions arose:

'What happened? Where is he?' *He* had disappeared. Maybe *he* was somewhere out in the garden, waiting for that second attack *he* had promised me.

'What a bastard to do that!'

'Yeah, bang out of order. I'll kill the fucker if I see him.'

'You've been cut, Sue.' Liam (not his real name) raised a hand towards my neck and drew it back with a trickle of blood. 'Don't know how he could've done that to you.'

'Let's make these ladies a cup of tea.' It was Jordan (again, not his real name) who spoke. Jordan who hated the system and everything in it and was always looking for an argument with it. 'Don't worry, Sue. You'll get loads of compensation for that – loads.'

A single police officer turned up and immediately sent for reinforcements. Managers were contacted, hyped-up residents milled about swearing they'd kill the bastard if they found him. There were the obligatory forms to fill out, questions to answer.

I borrowed a cigarette although I didn't normally smoke (in fact, I went through about ten borrowed cigarettes that night). I drew heavily on it and exhaled, pulled up the sleeve on my arm and stared at the bare skin, still scarred from decades-old self-harm cuts. I poised the cigarette ready to stab it out, to burn into my skin, to replace the hideous thing that had happened with another hideous but preferred pain of my own making. Because there were people there, I reluctantly stubbed it out in the ashtray instead.

It was a more senior policeman who noticed something was wrong. 'Are you hurt?' he asked me.

'I don't think so,' I said. I was on my feet, alive.

'You've been stabbed,' he said, pointing to my neck. It was a superficial cut, but I knew there were others.

'You need to go to the hospital to get checked out,' he said. 'That was a really nasty attack.'

Getting out of the vehicle and walking the few yards to the entrance of Accident and Emergency felt like an endless journey. All the way to the hospital I had scanned the road for signs of M. Inside the sliding doors of A & E, a violent car chase was taking place on television. I averted my gaze from it, trying to block out the loud noise – there had been enough violence for one night. My eyes kept reverting to the opening and shutting automatic doors. Nothing could stop him coming in if he was out there. It was a relief to be called down to be seen.

The male nurse in triage grimaced in disgust as I told him what had happened. He left me to wait for the doctor. I lay on a trolley in the cubicle and stared at the ceiling. I seemed to be somewhere else; the body on the bed seemed to belong to someone else. I lay for a long time before slipping off the bed and curling up against the wall, my head wrapped between my knees, the cold wall touching my spine through the hospital gown. I crouched once again into the foetal curl I had so recently emerged from, and slowly I began to rock backwards and forwards as a long moaning sound filled my head, a cry that seemed to be mourning for something irretrievably lost, for a world that would never be the same again.

I rocked for a long time. It was Saturday night and the staff were pushed to the limit. I hardly noticed the cold, hard floor and the wall pressing into my back, numbing my spine. Whoever was sitting there rocking on the floor was no longer me; I was somewhere else, indifferent to any physical pain. The strongest feeling that night was one of self-blame, a vague unspecified sense of having precipitated something horrendous.

As I rocked, something seemed to be taking more pity on me than I was on myself. At some point I must have registered that someone or something else was with me. There was no one physically there in the room, but I felt someone hovering – or rather a presence, which I seemed to know very well from somewhere but could not say where.

Where were you, then? I spoke to it in my head as one might speak to a friend who has turned up late for a meeting.

I was there with you, it said.

Bit bloody late.

I am always with you, it said. My mind flashed back to the point at which I seemed to have exited my body, occupying another space to the left of me. That was where I knew this being from. But I remembered it from other places throughout my life, in those moments when I felt I had reached the end of the road, when my back was totally against the wall. On this occasion it had been literally and metaphorically the case.

The rocking stopped. The horrible searing pain inside me abated. I climbed back on to the hospital trolley and heard the mourning cry inside me subside to a live whimper. Then it went quiet and still.

The young male Asian doctor who finally came to see me was kindness itself. Like the nurse, he expressed disgust at what had happened. He checked out the cuts and bruises that were starting to appear on my body, tutting at the emerging rainbow of colours across my stomach and chest and ribs and back, and at the bleeding red cuts from the knife. 'He should never have done that to you,' he murmured, half to himself, his face registering shame and disgust. I felt the solidarity from him that goes with working on the front line: a shared sense of vulnerability that goes on under the surface with the knowledge that you are always at risk from this kind of attack. Only it never happens. And if it does, it never happens to you.

He pressed gently on my aching ribs and swabbed at blood from the cuts. He arranged for a nurse to do some stitches. 'There's nothing broken,' he said, 'but I don't think this side of it is going to be the problem. Make sure your organisation gets you some help. You'll need it.'

He gave me a tube of spray to take away to use on the cuts. I treasured it like a present. In my broken, self-recriminating world, his kindness touched me deeply. I still have the spray at the back of a medicine cabinet – it is long out of date. He held the door open to me and said softly, 'Take care.'

I drove myself home at four o'clock in the morning. Ten miles away from the attack, I was still scanning the dark roads for signs of my attacker. He was out there somewhere and he had said he would kill me.

I locked the front door behind me and attached the chain. The dogs were delighted to see me home early and I had to deter them from jumping up at me as they usually did because the pressure on my skin hurt so much. I turned on the gas fire, placed a blanket in front of it and then curled underneath, fully clothed. Dessie nosed her way under the blanket too. I looked at her beautiful, innocent face, the dark button eyes with their eye-liner black rim around them contrasting with the whiteness of her forehead and muzzle. I buried my nose in her silky puppy ears and allowed her to snuggle into the foetal curl I was making. I winced at the pain from the pressure on my ribs, but for the first time that night I let out a long, long sigh of relief. She did not move for the rest of the night.

8

aftermath

The doorbell rang. My fist gripped around the bread knife in the kitchen. I walked slowly, deliberately, towards the door, the knife hanging half hidden behind my thigh. I could feel my teeth gritting, my eyes going hard. A primitive survival thought stood clearly in my mind:

I'll get him first this time.

It was him or me, and this time I'd be doing the killing.

I opened the door a fraction. A young woman stood outside.

'I'm the photographer from forensics,' she said. 'Is it all right to come in?' she added, noting that the door was still on the chain.

I nodded and let her in.

'I was just making a sandwich,' I said by way of explanation for the bread knife. In fact, I hadn't eaten for two days.

The dogs bounded up to greet her. She looked delighted. 'They're beautiful,' she laughed as Dessie jumped up to give her face a thousand licks. 'What are they called?'

I breathed a little. She liked dogs: she couldn't be all bad. She told me she was planning to get one, maybe a rescue dog, and asked me about dog care and management. I was happy to talk dogs – it postponed what was to follow.

She must have seen a lot of horrible sights in her time as a police photographer. She took pictures of the extensive bruising and cuts with quiet professionalism, only her mouth twisting in revulsion. The bruises were making a colourful display – purples and reds and blues. The yellows, greens and browns would come later, a rainbow of ugliness covering the white flesh – someone's white flesh: I didn't feel it belonged to me any more, and if it did, I no longer wanted it. But something intrigued me: a small circle of purple flesh, white in the centre.

'That's where he must have worn a ring,' she told me. 'That's one hell of a punch to do that.'

I stared at it. That punch had gone through four layers of clothing. I was sensitive to cold; if I hadn't been, the injuries would have been a lot worse. Some imprint from him had gone on to my body: he was still physically touching me. It was another reason to disown myself.

She collected the grim evidence and folded her equipment. 'I hope you feel better soon,' she said. I saw her to the door, without the bread knife.

A few minutes later I received a phone call from the senior police officer who had been at the scene, the one who had noticed something was wrong with me. He asked me how I was.

'You were very lucky,' he told me. 'You could easily have been killed. I didn't realise how bad it was until I spoke to your colleague.'

Lucky.

The word hovered over the line. Yes, I suppose I was. I was still standing, wasn't I?

There was a burning question I needed to ask.

'Have you… Has he been found yet?' There was a tremor in my voice.

'No,' he spoke gently. 'We've launched a massive manhunt in the area. We'll let you know as soon as anything happens. He'll be remanded immediately when we find him.'

When.

In the meantime he lurked somewhere outside my door. Perhaps he was already in the house, hiding somewhere, waiting to fulfil his final promise to me. I kept the bread knife waiting, ready for use, on the kitchen top, knowing that in all probability when he came – as I was convinced he would – I would be too paralysed to use it, too paralysed to move.

It seemed a lot of people wanted to contact me in the immediate aftermath of the attack. There were more police reports to go through; cards arrived from well-wishers in the Probation Service, most containing a hint of 'there but for the grace of whatever, we all go'. My boss rang me up, telling me not to come into work and filling me in on the situation with M who was still at large. The Chief Probation Officer for the county wrote, offering to help in any way he could.

They were written words coming through the letterbox. Inside, I was alone. No one came to see me and I did not go outside. The dogs subsisted on a quick run round the garden without me. I closed the door as soon as they were out, opening it as little as possible to let them back in. My attacker had transmuted into a superhuman force who could mysteriously know exactly where I was, how to enter my house through locked doors and solid stone walls. I had moved into the world of a horror movie; who knew what terror lurked under the bed, in the attic, down in the cellar? My logical capacity was no longer functioning; anything was possible and nowhere was safe.

The Probation Service had a contract with a counselling service, using counsellors across the region to provide support to people in the service. Behind the scenes, someone had arranged for one to ring me.

'I can offer you an appointment at the end of next week,' said a youngish female voice at the other end of the line.

End of next week. I fully expected to have been murdered by then.

'Where are you?' I asked.

She was several miles away.

'I don't feel I can leave the house at the moment.'

She spoke back in the terms of a professional offering seasoned advice: 'Those feelings usually go away in a few days.'

Something snapped. 'How the hell do you know what it feels like?' I demanded.

'Yes, I was told about what had happened to you,' she purred. 'It was awful, but it does get better.'

'How do you know?' I demanded again, furious and in no mood for bland, perfunctory reassurances that may or may not be true and which, in this case, I was 100 per cent certain weren't. I slammed the phone down and stared at the wall. For the first time, tears poured down my face, but I did not sob. Sobbing comes from within, a grief welling up, a connection with your own sorrow. I was not connected to anything inside myself any more. Like most people on the autistic spectrum, I can struggle to identify and process emotions. They happened somewhere inside me, but naming them was difficult. I was better at thinking things through than feeling. This was the case at the best of times, but now I had been blown into an unknown territory where the only emotion I felt certain of was terror.

In the days that followed I spent a lot of time staring into space. This could go on for several hours as I sat immobile in a slowly darkening room, only realising several hours later that it was dark and cold and that I was stiff from having stayed in the same position. I could not eat: food had become repugnant to me, a way of fuelling the body I no longer wished to be in or in fact *could* be in. It wasn't the self-denying hunger of anorexia, rather an inability to connect with all things of the flesh. My body felt damaged and violated and, since I had gone out of it on the night of the attack, no longer a place that I felt safe to return to.

And all the time danger was lurking. *He* was waiting for me, waiting to fulfil his promise:

I'm going to kill you.

He was there in the room. I was looking up, helpless, into the scarred, pockmarked face, the dead blue eyes with pinpoint pupils, the blue tinge of his shaven head. I could feel his supernatural strength, hear his freakily gentle voice. I was paralysed.

Dessie whined somewhere to the side of me. He mustn't hurt her; he could do what he wanted to me, but I would protect Dessie and all her puppyish innocence with my life.

A soft, dry tongue licked my hand; a cold, wet nose stuck itself into my palm. She whined again. My eyes flew open. She was there. He wasn't.

Shit!

I closed my eyes again and breathed out slowly. I was bathed in sweat. My hands, which cupped around Dessie's head, were shaking. Dessie jumped up beside me and nestled in my arms. I pushed my face into her soft, silky neck; my breathing was coming short and fast. Slowly I realised I was back in the room awake and there was a warm, sentient, non-threatening being with me. Poppy climbed up on the bed, lying on top of me. I winced as her weight pressed against my injuries but I did not move away. I wanted to feel connected to something alive and warm and safe.

This time it had been a nightmare. Another one: I had them every night, often several times. But I didn't have to be asleep for him to be there. He was there, sometimes in the house, sometimes waiting outside. He would never leave me.

In my isolation, there was no one to contradict the flaws in my thinking, to bring me out of the traumatised space I was now living in. As I alternately swung between staring into space in frozen immobility or being jolted into a state of hyper-vigilance, watching and waiting for my attacker to reappear, only the dogs could bring me back into a temporary reality. Their physical demands for food, water and exercise had to be met. This meant moving, touching physical objects, having a plan and a purpose for however short a space of time. This grounded me for the duration.

I stayed alone in the house. I had told no one about what had happened – there were few enough people that I could tell anyway and a lifetime habit of near silence about my inner state could not be easily broken. The organisation I worked for had also gone silent. No one had been to see me and after the first few days no one had rung me to ask if I was all right. Perhaps the assumption was that I would draw around me all the usual support mechanisms of family and friends and neighbours, which perhaps those in the 'other world' could expect or take for granted. But, as always, I was on my own. And I was in trouble.

Something had happened to me that I could only relate back to the point of the assault at which I had exited or dissociated from my body. At the time I had been outside myself, looking on, witnessing what appeared to be my imminent murder. The murder had not happened, but I had not gone back inside myself; I was still outside looking in.

In exiting myself, I had taken all my resources with me: I could not think or feel or function properly. My energies seemed to have become engaged in a kind of animal survival mechanism. I had entered a kill-or-be-killed world where the bread knife lay poised on the kitchen worktop ready to attack. I could not eat because I was also poised, ready to run, and to eat would be a distraction, a slowing-down process. Another part of me, the part that sat frozen still for hours at a time, was caught in a headlight glare, unable to move. I veered daily between the three primitive states of Fight, Flight or Play Dead.

And I didn't know what to do. Although I had often been dissociated from the world around me, I had used my private self as a sanctuary. It had been my safe haven, the only one I had had, but now I seemed to have been blasted out of it and all the inner resources which protected me had gone. It struck me as the ultimate irony that I who had spent all my life building defences to keep the outer world at bay, who could be oblivious to any crowd or social situation by resorting to an obsessive thought chain, could do nothing against this invasion by someone who effectively was no longer there. I looked at the books overflowing the book shelves, spilling out of the cupboards. All of them were useless. When it came down to it, all my thinking, all the learning I had acquired over the years had been reduced to a primitive survival response. I was operating at an animal level.

9

consequences

I had to leave the house but it was no longer a simple matter. To get from my house to the doctor's appointment, a mere ten minutes' drive away, had become a protracted process. For many minutes I sat psyching myself up to leave, willing myself to exchange the frozen immobility that I'd become accustomed to for the normal action of getting into the car and driving somewhere. The minutes ticked by; I was going to be late.

Drawing on a lifetime habit of having to meet the times of others, I began to act. First, the bread knife had to be removed from the kitchen to just inside the doorway in a nook under the staircase. If I came back and *he* was here, I would need to grab it quickly. Second, I had to check the street. From behind curtains that had not been drawn for days, I looked out at a side angle, from which I felt reasonably sure no one could see me, and surveyed the street. If anyone was there, I would have to wait until they'd gone and then check again and then check from the opposite side of the window. All clear and I could go out. Perhaps. Better to go back and just double-check and, whilst I was at it, double-check that the back door was locked and chained, even though, like the curtains, it had not been open for days. How easy would it be to break down that locked and chained door if you had superhuman strength? How many places could you hide in a one-bedroomed cottage when you could walk through walls? And what if I simply forgot to lock the front door and he just walked in?

It was probably like trying to make your way across the room with a newly broken leg, having to rethink each move to minimise pain. Except with a broken leg you expect it will get better at some point, and sometimes someone will hold the door open for you.

I arrived for my appointment ten minutes late. A frosty receptionist gave me a frosty reception and told me that doctors had a strict appointment schedule and I would have to wait until a slot was free. I gave her a dirty look and pointed out that I had yet to find a doctor on the NHS who was capable of working to time anyway. She blushed with annoyance. I did not care. I was on the offensive; my fight mechanism had kicked in and was working overtime.

The young female doctor who saw me was gentle and kind and the complete antithesis of the receptionist. I needed a sick note because I could not return to work. She listened as I outlined what had happened, her face registering the same repugnance as the doctor at the hospital and, again, that mutual sympathy of those in the firing line, always vulnerable, but mercifully rarely on the receiving end of an attack.

'Your work should arrange some help for you,' she said. 'That sounds like a very serious assault.' I didn't tell her that I had sat in a silent house for days. She prescribed me some Prozac (it was the beginning of a long and, on the whole, beneficial relationship with the drug) and insisted I come back. I felt that what had happened to me mattered to someone else and in my current state that had a particular significance. I had lost my inner self on the night of the attack; it was out there somewhere but I had no access to it, and in my isolation I felt I needed something or someone to help me. I did not have the resources to deal with this terrifying new state alone. In my doctor I had found an ally. Perhaps it was only for the brief space of time in her office but it was something.

I returned to my cold, dark house and waited alone.

The silence from work continued and doubtless would have carried on if a female work colleague had not broken rank and rung me up to see how I was.

'I'm really sorry,' she prefaced her enquiry over the phone. 'I just needed to know if you were all right. We've been told not to contact you, but I had to just ask.'

I stared at the phone. I had been alone for days with no one and they had been told not to contact me. Later I came up with two possible explanations, one charitable, one more cynical. My charitable explanation was that perhaps it was an act of kindness, a way of giving me space to recover, based, as I have said, on the assumption that I was being looked after by somebody out there. My second explanation, which was partly borne out later, was that it was the usual back-covering exercise of a paranoid public service organisation, an attempt to make sure that nothing was said that could lead to future recriminations. I'm still not wholly sure if either one was right.

But there was one more piece of information that was conveyed to me before near total silence descended. The colleague who rang me mentioned it casually:

'Well, I suppose it all feels a bit different now that he's dead...'

'He's *what*?' I stared at the phone again, not understanding what I was hearing.

'You mean you didn't know?'

'Didn't know what?' I demanded.

'I'm sorry,' she said. 'I thought you'd been told. He was found dead of a heroin overdose in a flat.'

My attacker was dead.

That was what she was saying and yet that couldn't be right. He was out there, waiting to kill me. I knew he was.

I listened, bewildered, as she spelled out what details she knew. He had been found in a flat in Bradford and identified by the tattoos on his knuckles. It was him, and he had been dead since either the night of the attack or the day after. And yet why had he been lurking outside, waiting to kill me? Why had I known that he was somewhere in the house? The whys flooded in. It wasn't making any sense.

Later I sat frozen again, staring at the wall in the darkened, fireless room, playing over the meaningless words in my head: *He's dead.*

If he was dead, who or what had killed him? What caused him to overdose? Was it a case of bad gear? Too much too soon on a system that had detoxed in prison? Or was it the knowledge that to attack someone in a law-enforcement profession such as probation would carry the heaviest of sentences? If it came to court, he would have risked having the book thrown at him. The only possible outcome was a long prison sentence; having been in the system for years, M would have known this. Did he take his own life to avoid it?

One thing was certain: now I would never know and his death hung over me more heavily than the assault itself. If I hadn't spoken to him, hadn't hauled him into the office to challenge his behaviour, none of this might have happened: M might not be dead and my work colleague on that night might not be going through something similar to this.

Next day my boss rang me.

'I believe you've heard what happened,' he said. 'I was going to come and tell you myself.' He sounded weary, as if the whole sordid business had caught up with him. He told me he was going away on holiday for a week.

That was the last I heard from the organisation until they decided it was time for me to come back to work.

I was sitting in the car in the supermarket car park and my teeth were chattering. It was a warm spring evening and the light was just starting to fade. When it was fully dark, I would do it, I told myself: drive the car into the high wall of solid Yorkshire stone at the edge of the car park. It stood there, a barrier between me and oblivion.

I had parked the car several feet away, enough distance to get up speed. It wouldn't take much, I reasoned it through: just a few quick revs on the accelerator, clutch into gear, foot down, handbrake off – as easy as learning those first few steps of driving. And then it would all stop.

The bruising and cuts on my body could be replaced by other bruises and cuts, perhaps broken bones, perhaps oblivion. And there would be one major difference: any more damage done to me would be damage of my own creation, not the infliction of an alien outsider who had invaded my world and sent me spinning out of it, left only to look on the empty shell that I had become. The physical hurt was largely irrelevant; it was the unseen damage and the guilt that I could not deal with.

With the self-harmer's logic, I wanted to replace one kind of hurt with another, and the more it hurt, the better; the more it competed against the inner damage and superseded it, the better. Maybe that was why I had wanted to stub out the cigarette on my bare flesh on the night of the attack – physical hurt was different: it would heal eventually, or kill you, and in the meantime it would replace this hurt that I felt would never heal.

The shadows in the car park were lengthening. The neon from the store and the street lamps dotted around began to light up the parking bays, the rows of trolleys. The stone wall fell into shadow. I watched as families of shoppers loaded up the boots of their cars, returned trolleys to the trolley park, drove home to normal family lives which I would never share. I did not envy them as a rule; at best I was highly ambivalent. Other people had their lives and I had mine, and I was more comfortable in my isolation than I ever was around others, the notion or concept of family or wider social contact conjuring up images of paralysing restriction and an overload of sensory stimuli. In the social context I had always been an outsider looking in, but it was not altogether the looking in of a child with its nose pressed against a sweetshop window, a window that stood between the haves and have-nots. I had my own rich resources, the infinite space of the inner world. Until now. And I did not envy the outer world. Until now.

I watched the outer world going about its business, imagined them around dinner tables and fires and TVs, eating, talking;

not alone, not afraid, not responsible for injuries caused to a work colleague who had risked everything to help them, not guilty of possible murder, not sitting here, planning how it could all be over. And I wished I was part of it.

No one had accused me of anything, Perhaps they were all being kind, treating me in my injured state with kid gloves, the whispers going on somewhere behind hands: 'It's her fault.' And somehow I knew it was: I had been central to all this, and the blame for injury and death must lie somewhere. And, besides, my dreams were telling me I was guilty.

M had ceased to stand over me before I awoke, threatening to kill me, but his mother had taken his place – an elderly lady in grey, with loose strands of grey hair falling around her withered face, speaking as if from the dead, but still a mother grieving for her dead son.

'He's dead,' she said in my dreams. 'And it's your fault.' The silence that followed was chilling. I could not reply, could not defend myself, even if there was any defence to produce. I wanted to say I was sorry, beg for forgiveness, explain that it could not have been helped. But as always, even in my dreams, words choked inside me, buried so deep they would never be dredged up into daylight. So I awoke convicted in a Kafkaesque world where a different logic ruled.

Time was ticking on. The families had gone home to their normality. A few solitary shoppers were coming out with carrier bags. I looked at the stone wall. My teeth began to chatter again and I turned the key in the ignition, the engine softly kicking into life. My hand on the gear stick was shaking as I rocked it from side to side in neutral. I hovered a tentative foot over the accelerator. The gear stick continued to push to and fro in my sweating hand.

Do it! I swore to myself between gritted teeth.

Go on! Do it!

My foot made a tentative rev and then retreated as if of its own accord. I tried again. And again. I let go of the gear stick and slumped back in the seat. My body had gone weak and unresponsive, as if all the power had been drained. I stared at the wall, knowing all it would take would be one push of the gear stick, a few fast revs, release the handbrake; that was all that stood between me and oblivion, complete escape from this hideous feeling inside me. And I knew I couldn't do it. Something in me still wanted to survive: the same part of me that had internally pleaded for my remaining unlived life on the night of the attack. For all that I had spent so many of my young adult years in an endless inner debate about the pros and cons of suicide, I had come out firmly on the side of the living.

Pathetic bitch!

Sometime later, when it was fully dark, I drove home, back to the hunger and the cold and the nightmares. In the hallway, the bread knife was lying in its new home. I looked at someone in the mirror who used to be me. I stared and a stranger stared back, not knowing where I had gone or who or what remained.

10

to the lighthouse

There was quite a bit of advice around about what to do. None of it useful. Word about what had happened had got out to the small circle of people who knew me and suggestions, well-meant but with no grasp of the reality of my situation, poured in: try reading, write about it, get yourself a decent meal, try counselling, go on holiday, sue the arse off the Probation Service; you'll be a stronger person when you come through; time heals…

Actually, time doesn't heal in the traumatised world. By definition, you are stuck at the point of trauma, unable to process what has happened and either condemned to repeatedly live as if the life-threatening experience were still a current reality or destined to block it out and allow it to take on a life of its own, wreaking its own particular brand of havoc at will. And one thing was certain as I stayed in this alien world: I could see no way out or forward now that I had moved into a whole new different territory. I continued to veer between primitive fight, flight or freeze modes which segued relentlessly into each other.

Maybe that was why I still could not eat. For the first week after the attack I barely ate at all; any food I raised to my mouth would be left to fall. Perhaps it was because eating slows you down, makes the body heavier and unable to perform at its best when flight is required. The possible need to take flight showed no signs of going away and weeks of living off caffeine-fuelled drinks and less than 400 calories a day were starting to catch up on me. My hands showed it first as the bones on the back of them started to stick out. Altogether I was to lose one-third of my body weight.

Hunger didn't help my mental functioning either. I longed for the old comfort of being able to escape into reading, of losing myself in a fictional world, but my mind would not focus. It was little wonder really when the rest of me was poised ready for flight at the slightest threat. Small sounds made me jumpy: a knock on the door (not that there were many), the dogs barking suddenly or a voice in the street all signalled a very real potential threat. I remained in a state of hyper-vigilance in a battle zone where the bread knife remained ready and waiting on the kitchen work surface and the curtains remained drawn against a threatening exterior world.

Fear had made me hyper-alert but I also felt anger. The fight-or-flight mechanism was equipoised within me, and if I couldn't take flight if I were cornered, I would have no choice but to fight. Sometimes rage seared through me at a perceived stare, a mistimed piece of advice; on the rare occasions I went out, anyone coming too close to me would be the butt of it: silent furious rage. If there was a threat, this time I was determined that I would get in first and ask questions later. It was a wild, savage kind of anger – the kind of anger that might be expected from an injured dog. At other times I felt afraid, anxious to placate for any wrongdoing, real or imaginary, that I might have committed. After all, I was on a suspected murder charge in my head. Maybe the verdict would never come but the charge still hung over me.

The reality was that I needed and wanted something but didn't know what. My autism had never allowed me to reach out and ask; there was no ingrained expectation that anyone would give me something or owed me anything. With autism, you are in the truest sense on your own with whatever life throws at you. My preferred coping mechanism for dealing with what life had thrown at me so far was withdrawal into my private self and burying into obsessive reading, but now I didn't seem to have a private self left to withdraw into and I was no longer able to read. Inside the house, the cold, hungry house, I continued to stare at the walls and wait. Whatever I needed would have to come from outside the autistic bubble.

Word had filtered out and one day I received a phone call from a friend I had known briefly some months previously. Sue had moved with her partner Frederica up to a lighthouse on the east coast of Scotland to pursue her career as a poet and author. Always sociable, she offered me the chance to come up and stay for a few days. I wondered if a change of scenery might not just offer me the break I needed, a chance to step back from what had happened, to breathe again. A lighthouse on a remote Scottish coast sounded like autistic heaven.

'I'm in a bit of a strange place at the moment,' I said. 'I might not talk or eat much.'

She told me not to worry. The place was at my disposal, no strings attached. They would both be out at work all day anyway.

Going outside of my front door was a challenge but once inside the locked doors of the car I seemed to be able to function – at least enough to drive to a destination. I always liked being alone in the metal capsule of the car; it was a private world in itself and I could still go into it – as long, that is, as all four doors were locked. I dropped the dogs off at the kennels and drove to Scotland, to Aberdeenshire on the east coast.

The decommissioned lighthouse stood on a cliff above a rocky, pebbled beach, looking out on to the North Sea. It was mid-spring and bleak in a way that only a north British spring can be, the grey leaden skies meeting the grey North Sea in endless monotone.

I sat alone on the beach and watched the crashing waves surging and retreating again in what Arnold described in *Dover Beach* as their 'melancholy, long, withdrawing roar'. As I watched, it seemed like a pointless repetition, a dull beating of and withdrawing from the shingle. Normally, I liked the sea, the endless possibilities that its unlimited horizons suggested, the isolated majesty and the often understated but limitless potential power. As a child at school, the sounds of seagulls flying inland from the Irish Sea coast had always thrilled me, their mournful cries suggesting another world somewhere else – true, it was probably a world more redolent of a 'dirty British coaster' than the 'quinquireme of Nineveh', but it spoke of places other than the confines of a hated boring classroom and because it wasn't *there* (and anywhere was always better than *there*), it seemed infinitely preferable.

But here as I watched the pointless repetition of the waves, a dull beating of and withdrawing from the shingle, the gull calls had become a hollow, mocking caw, and the birds themselves were merely scavengers, a dull, dreary part of a monotonous world. I stared out at the limitless horizon and saw only grey limitation. Behind me, the decommissioned lighthouse stood facing the pointless battering waves, solitary, unused, with the light turned out forever. My journey to the lighthouse was going to be no final act of redemption or reconciliation, and Woolf's final chapter stood in my head like a mockery – I felt more as if I was living in the unreal world of a gothic horror fantasy.

I stayed for a few days and then returned home. Sue and Frederica had been as good as their word, imposing nothing on me, prepared to let me just be there. When I wasn't sitting on the beach, I lay on the couch and stared at the wall. On the night before I left, Frederica said to me, 'I don't know what you can do to get over this.'

It was honest at least, amidst false promises and truisms from well-meaning people who did not understand what was happening.

I drove back home to be swept with more 'confused alarms of struggle and flight'. One thing was certain: it was going to take more, much more, than a change of outer landscape to transform the inner wilderness inside me and, for the first time ever, literature was offering no consolation.

I had never felt much attachment to my physical surroundings – living mainly in an interior world, it was easy to remain oblivious to them. In my more restless years I had lived out of carrier bags and unpacked boxes for months, never putting down any roots, but now that I had achieved my own house and the mortgage to prove it, I did try to make a bit of an effort when I remembered.

Back home, however, I felt detached from my surroundings in a different way. The house and everything in it remained untouched, slowly accumulating dust and dog hair. I watched it from a frozen, detached distance. What did it have to do with me anyway if I wasn't properly there? Despite knowing what had happened to my attacker, I wasn't able to process it. Something inside me believed he was still out there, alive, waiting to get me, and therefore I might need to flee at any moment. Under the circumstances, the dusting could wait and, besides, I lacked any spare energy: my weight was plummeting rapidly. When I was not sitting, frozen, staring at the wall, I had taken to sleeping for hours, not wanting to wake. I still had nightmares (they would continue for a long time), but sleeping usually meant a long period of oblivion, and oblivion was what I craved most.

It was still only the dogs who regularly caused me to come out of this state. Not only did their needs have to be met but they had taken it upon themselves to bring me back to earth if I seemed to have drifted off too far or for too long. Dessie in particular would come up and lick my hand, force her head on my lap and look up at me with her black-rimmed eyes which I always found too beautiful to ignore. Often she would give me that characteristic Dalmatian smile (it looks like a snarl but is a submissive, ingratiating gesture) and it always made me smile back or laugh, no matter how bad I was feeling. Dalmatians are amongst the most tactile of dogs and a known characteristic of theirs is to lie across people's knees, given half a chance. They are a kind of lapdog manqué, far too big and boisterous to be doing that, but anyone who has ever tried to tell a Dalmatian what it can and can't do knows it is a losing battle. In my frozen isolation it was probably one of the best things that could happen to me – it brought me back to something live and warm, something I could place my hand on and feel the soft fibres of the coat, look at the spotted pattern, smell that warm dog smell. It reconnected me with my senses, which brought me back, if only briefly, into the present moment, and it was done by them at times when I was incapable of reaching out from myself. Living in a state of permanent high stress, the rhythmic act of stroking calmed me down; when I looked at the dogs, I caught myself smiling. Sometimes I spoke to them, hearing my voice again after long hours of silence. Sometimes I just sat or lay with them and did nothing, and they demanded nothing more of me.

Years later I learned about how service dogs working with war veterans suffering from post-traumatic stress disorder are trained to ground their owners by jumping up or gaining their attention when the veterans revert back to the traumatising event in their heads and become dissociated from current reality. Dogs also provide a focus, a live being to care for that is non-threatening and which can make them feel safe when going into new situations, or simply in some cases being able to go through their front door.

Poppy and Dessie did this for me independently, providing a link, however temporary, with the world I had become doubly shut off from due to trauma and autism. I doubt that I would ever have gone out voluntarily during that time, but two big, active Dalmatians still needed walking. All walks were brief and stressful, but going out was made much easier because I felt safer with them. They were big striking dogs – any attention would most likely go to them first and, in this unsafe world I was occupying, they would surely act as a deterrent to any attacker. In reality, the biggest danger any attacker would probably face would be being licked to death by the world's soppiest dogs. Still, a small illusion can be useful.

Most of the time, however, I remained inside, the bread knife ready and waiting and the dust rising. The irony was not lost on me that I had once happily travelled the world on my own and that only a few months earlier I had been planning to go halfway round it again on the Trans-Siberian Express from Moscow to Beijing. Now I did not want to cross my own doorstep and, when I did, I could not wait to get back inside.

11

a journey begins

It was a hot day in the health centre. I was there because my sick note had run out and I needed a new Prozac prescription, and I did not want to be there. I sat in the annex part which was built like a conservatory; hot days in Yorkshire are not all that common and the ill-conceived conservatory was baking. I had been there for an 11 o'clock appointment and it was now a quarter to 12. I would have found the wait difficult at the best of times – a certain literalness in me thought that 11 o'clock meant 11 o'clock, no matter how many times experience had taught me otherwise. Add to that the fact that I desperately wanted to get back to the safe interior of the four walls of my house and my insides were beginning to rage.

I needed to go home, needed to be alone behind closed doors again. To add insult to injury, the inane drivel of a local radio station was invading my head, jarring on my ears and shattering the silence I had been living in for weeks. I looked with angry contempt at what I regarded as the trashy lifestyle magazines on the tables. Is that what we were supposed to read and listen to, courtesy of the NHS which couldn't get its act together to make sure appointments ran to time? Normally,

I would have brought a book with me to block out the noise, the presence of others, the rising sense of panic and stress that waiting in such places brought out in me. But now it was pointless. I hadn't read a book for weeks. I sat fuming as my stress levels rose through the conservatory glass roof.

At 12.05 my name was called out. It was the same pleasant young doctor who had seen me originally. She smiled a welcome. 'What a lovely day.'

'Yes and I don't want to be spending it in here,' I snapped, even more angry that there had been no explanation or apology.

Her face fell and a look of contrition passed across it. 'I'm really sorry to have kept you waiting,' she said. 'It's been very busy, so everything's behind.'

I expected to get the usual three minutes of NHS doctor's time – a perfunctory enquiry as to how I was, a repeat prescription printed off, a reluctant invitation to come back 'if you feel you need to'. It would probably have been justified, given the mood I was in, but, bypassing my spikey, angry response, she invited me to sit down.

'You've been having a really tough time, haven't you?' Her gentleness caught me off my guard, melted me. It was something I had never expected. I found myself talking about what was happening – the nightmares, the inability to eat, fear of going outside the house…

'That's why I didn't want to be here so long,' I said, feeling slightly remorseful about my earlier response.

'I don't blame you,' she said. 'I hate waiting in these places too.'

She encouraged me to talk and for once I felt myself able to. I told her about how I seemed to have gone out of myself, how I no longer wanted to occupy the devastated territory that was my body, how I hated seeing the bruising and scars still covering it, how everything seemed to be in ruins and felt as if it would never be the same again.

Then she asked me a question: 'What do you like doing where you have to get out and about and mix with people?'

It was a simple enough question but I found it hard to answer. Prior to the attack I had mainly lived in my internal world, reading and thinking and, as technology advanced, becoming more engrossed in the internet. I didn't really 'get out and do things'. That seemed to imply having someone to do them with and for me that was rarely the case. I racked my brains.

'I walk the dogs,' I said at last.

'That's something you have to do,' she pressed. 'What about something you just enjoy doing, like swimming or cycling?'

Swimming was out. I disliked the cold clinical tiles of public pools, the smell of chlorine, cold water and, most of all, having to mix with strange people. And I was still a mass of bruises weeks after the attack – not something you want displayed in public. Cycling was a possibility. Before moving to Yorkshire, I had cycled a lot in Oxford and Oxfordshire – it was one way to beat the horrendous parking costs. But Oxford was probably the most bike-friendly town in the country then and many of the roads were relatively flat. The Yorkshire moors and proximity to the Pennines required a level of fitness I could no longer summon up, especially on the limited food rations I was getting. Besides, the roads could be manic and the drivers homicidal when it came to cyclists.

She suggested other options such as joining a gym or interest group. I never bothered to explain to people why I didn't feel as if I fitted in or belonged anywhere – explaining your solitary status in a predominantly social world is never easy – so I just shook my head. To be quite honest, I lacked the motivation to do anything that would help. I didn't really believe anything would and, apart from that, guilt over everything I seemed to have caused left me feeling that I didn't deserve to feel better.

'What about aromatherapy or a massage session to get you back inside yourself?' my doctor persisted. I shook my head again. I didn't want anyone to come into the space around me at the best of times – autism carried with it a *Strictly No Entry* sign. In any case, I was still too physically sore to want any additional pressure on me.

'You said you had dogs,' she said. 'Do you like animals?'

It was one of those innocent, chance questions that can change a whole life, though neither of us knew it at the time. I thought for a moment, memories stirring. Horses had once been my overriding obsession, occupying my every waking moment as a child and quite a few sleeping ones as well.

'I used to like horses…' I said.

She smiled. 'I love horses. They're amazing, aren't they?'

I don't know how or when my love affair with horses began. It seemed it had always been there – innate, unquestionable, enduring and impossible to explain. I've since discussed this many times with horse people who feel the same, but no one seems quite able to pinpoint the cause. One thing, however, is certain: there is no cure.

As far back as I can remember, horses obsessed me. I loved their multiple forms, from Shetlands to Shires, their beauty, their power, their speed and grace, and that ultimate unknowable quality that each one carries. As a child, I studied books and pictures of horses endlessly, scribbling over any human presence which would invariably spoil it for me (a twentieth-century child's version of airbrushing). *The Observer's Book of Horses and Ponies* came into my possession when I was seven and I spent hours admiring the beauty of the palomino, the Mohican cut of the Fjord's mane, the hacks, hunters, thoroughbreds and cobs that peopled my imagination day and night. Once, many years later, I came across the same book on someone's book shelf. The owner had at one time drawn saddles and bridles on her favourite pictures and given the horses names like Rocky and Starlight and Thunder. I know exactly why she did that.

I read endlessly about the pony world. There was a strong line of pre- and post-war pony fiction around by children's authors such as the Pullein-Thompson sisters. The stories described a lost world occupied by people with double-barrelled surnames, retired colonels and the honourable so-and-sos running Pony Clubs for well-to-do children. Usually, the stories culminated in the righteous girls being presented with a rosette by the local squire's wife at the village gymkhana – that's assuming the righteous girls weren't common (for that, read working class). One thing was clear: to have a pony, you probably needed to be rich too.

A girl's obsession with horses is not overly unusual, but I took it to a rather extreme level – the fact that the actual object of it was missing in reality was no obstacle. I avidly learned the points of the horse, parts of the tack, illnesses, breeds… In the absence of the real thing, I temporarily transferred my obsession to cows. It was a poor substitute but, like horses, cows lived in fields, ate grass, had four legs, and at a pinch you could pretend a Friesian cow was a piebald horse. I probably only saw cows once a week when being driven to church on Sundays, but it was fuel for my obsession for the rest of the week.

When I was about six, I spent my pocket money buying a plastic, gold-covered horse with a white mane and tail for my mother's birthday present. I couldn't think of a nicer present for anyone. Sometime later, when I asked her if I could keep it in my room, my mother (who disliked all animals) said yes – I don't think parting with it was too much of a wrench for her. I stuck it on the bedstead with Blu-Tack and it joined the other herd of ponies in the bedroom: plastic, ceramic, pictures on the wall, in books…everything except the real thing. When the local pet shop started selling tack and grooming gear, it was additional fuel for my obsession. Hours spent watching rabbits and goldfish and terrapins were replaced by hours looking at curry combs and hoof picks and parts of a saddle and bridle. I secretly bought a hoof pick and a mane comb. Although I never expected I would ever have the chance to use them, I felt that in some way they brought me a bit closer to the horse world. I hid them at the bottom of a treasure box; the hoof pick is still there today, unused.

As I grew older, I did occasionally manage to ride at a pony-trekking centre set up on the nearby Pennines. Rides were fast and furious, and I fell off virtually every time, but that was fine – it was a small price to pay. I didn't get to go very often, but the times I did filled my memories for weeks after. When I was 12, I had a few lessons at a riding school with the proviso from my mother that if I fell off once there wouldn't be any more. I didn't fall off but the lessons were stopped after a few weeks on the basis that I needed to concentrate on my school work (effectively, no one could be bothered to take me). That half hour a week was clearly set to ruin my glittering academic career.

To say I was obsessed is an understatement. Eventually, horses receded from my life, not because I gave up on them but because the opportunity to experience them simply wasn't there.

Although my childhood obsession with horses had become a dim and distant memory by the time I came to talk to the doctor, my link with horses had never quite gone away. Even then, I could never pass a herd in a field without stopping to look, still entranced by their beauty and power, intrigued by their behaviour, expressions, colours and smells. The sound of horses' hooves, their rhythmic beat, always arrested me, and I still consider it to be one of the most beautiful sounds in the world – up there with Bach and the cry of nightingales and the clinking of ice cubes in whisky. The whole extensive paraphernalia that goes with the horse world – stables, tack, hay – exerted an inexplicable hold on me.

As an adult, I had occasionally gone riding when I could afford it, but this was too infrequent for me to make any real progress and I had reached a point at which I had consigned it to one of those things I would never be any good at. Still, if I ever dreamt about the perfect place to live, it was always in the middle of nowhere with enough land to keep horses (significantly, there was never any thought of a spare room for friends or guests).

I briefly outlined some of this to my doctor. She had clearly experienced a similar obsession and I felt that she needed no convincing of the strange, intangible hold that horses exert on some people. She simply smiled a knowing smile and said, 'I want you to go away and book a riding lesson, and then come back in a week, or however long it takes, and tell me how it went.'

It was somewhere between an order and a piece of advice. I found myself agreeing.

A journey was about to begin.

12

the horse effect

As I sat at home and reverted to my usual state of frozen paralysis, I doubted if I would follow through with the agreement. But two things pushed me: first, there was the fact that I was still inexorably drawn to horses; second, I'd been told (however kindly) to do it and I had a tendency to do what other people told me if I felt well disposed towards them. The doctor had been kind to me. She had given me some time, so I felt that on some level I owed it to her to try it, even if it was just a one-off that I would never repeat. Maybe I was also trying to override the stalemate I had been in since the night of the attack. I wanted things to change; I just had no idea how this was going to happen.

I looked up riding schools in the phone book. There were quite a few in rural Yorkshire, a contrast to their virtual non-existence when I was growing up in urban Lancashire. Just looking at them in the directory took me back to those feelings of exclusion from the only thing in the world I had really wanted to be a part of, and a voice in my head said – as voices in your head will – *Isn't it a bit late in the day to be doing this? You're not a kid any more.*

But the doctor had been kind to me, so I would do it once and that would be it. Slowly, deliberately, I dialled a number.

'Na then,' said a gruff, male voice. *Na then* is Yorkshire; it has various meanings and in this case roughly translated as 'What can I do for you?'

'Is that the riding school?' I asked, puzzled.

'Aye, lass. 'Ang aboot, she's owt wit 'orses. I'll go ger 'er for you.' I was liking this already. It was a far cry from the double-barrelled Clarissas and Lucindas of the Pony Club world I had read about when growing up.

'Er picked up the phone. ''Ello, love, 'ow can I 'elp you?'

I asked about booking a lesson.

'Can't do owt this month, love – school's bin flooded. I'll give you't number for someone as can 'elp.'

'Oh, thanks.' I wrote the number down and redialled. This time the ménage hadn't been flooded and my lesson was duly booked. I just had to turn up.

Therein lay the rub.

On the morning of the ride I hesitated as always before going out of the door. The usual rituals had to be gone through. Check back door is locked with chain on (actually, it was never unlocked or unchained these days), check all windows are shut (again, none was ever opened), see if you can see anyone in street from behind curtains and, if so, wait until all clear. Move knife from kitchen to under the stairs by front door. On approach to front door, have keys ready in hand to get straight into car. Better still, think twice: is this journey really necessary? If not, abandon and stay at home.

It was all about as pointless as dancing widdershins around a bonfire on a full moon, but in strange times we adopt strange superstitions; there are no certainties left to draw on.

I arrived at the riding stables with no minutes to spare, but as I've yet to come across a riding school that ran to time and no one seemed to be about, I had a few moments to look around. It was a large outfit of about 40 stables, with a big indoor arena and a parking area filled with horse trailers and wagons. It stood on top of a windswept hill on a Yorkshire moor. After living in cities where every spare millimetre of land seemed to be accounted for, fenced off and probably mortgaged to the hilt, the spaciousness of Yorkshire never ceased to amaze me. Around me I had that wonderful 360-degree vision of the surrounding fields and moors and dry stone walls. Spring was coming in reluctantly and the fields were still more yellow-brown than green at this exposed and rugged height. I breathed deeply – surely no one would come looking for me here. Or would they?

I leaned against a fence overlooking the fields and took in the panorama, feeling my aloneness. This wasn't *loneliness* – I had no real concept of what that meant, when to be alone felt as natural as breathing and to be with others often felt as unnatural as choking. It had more to do with entering the social world, even though, as on this occasion, it was voluntary. At such times I always felt my outsider status, but these days I felt I had acquired another status too – that of victim. I felt fragile and vulnerable in a way I never had before. Being on the autistic spectrum, I could never assume that anyone would be there to help me, take my side or fight my corner, with the consequence that I had become highly self-reliant and independent. If I needed to do something or go somewhere, I would do it without ever having to seek approval or permission, and over the years I had come to see myself as a self-determining, self-sufficient and resourceful individual. Now that the person I had been had gone out of me and I no longer had my inner self to retreat back into, I felt as if I was operating without any stable base. One perceived negative look or word and I might crumble. Maybe it was because I was still covered in physical injuries too. In the wild I would have been an easy target for any passing predator; hence I was like a prey animal poised for flight. For all the open freedom before me, I was locked in a prison of fear and hurt and vulnerability.

But I had got here and I would go through with it.

I followed a wooden sign saying 'Office', which led to a converted stable doubling up as a chicken run and dog kennel. Stroking a large Alsatian behind its ears made me feel a bit calmer, and a girl behind a desk smiled and told me I was on Charlie. I was duly fitted with a riding hat and went off to meet him 'down the barn at the end'. Walking through the American barn with rows of horses stabled on either side, I breathed deeply again. The smell was intoxicating – that combination of straw and hay and boozy, tobacco-smelling haylage mingled with the odour of horse sweat, ammonia, manure, the sweet, special smell of horses and the hint of leather from tack. It was olfactory heaven. OK, so it will never end up as a bestseller on the Boots counters, but those of us who love horses know what it is, know that nothing smells sweeter. And if you *could* bottle it, we'd buy it.

I looked over the stable doors at the horses. It was like my *Observer Book of Horses and Ponies* come to life: there were all kinds and shapes, from a cheeky little chestnut Shetland to massive working hunters, thoroughbreds and cobs. I was entranced and, as always with animals but never with humans, I was drawn towards them, going up to their stable doors and reaching my hand over to pat them or to breathe into their nostrils, or simply to murmur quietly to them. I would probably have stayed all day doing this if someone hadn't called me and introduced me to Charlie. Charlie was a 13-hands piebald cob and didn't look too intimidating. I liked him instantly – cobs tend to be amongst the less complicated of horses, being governed largely by the need to eat to keep their considerable body weight going. Charlie was tacked up and stood chewing nonchalantly on his bit whilst I stroked him, enjoying the soft velvet feel of his pink and white muzzle on my hands. He nuzzled my pockets, but I had nothing to give him and silently berated myself for it. He was led into the indoor school and stood beside a mounting block, where he waited patiently as I struggled to get on, long out of practice, and for the stirrup leathers and girth to be adjusted.

'How much riding have you done?' the instructor asked me.

I told her about my chequered involvement with horses. 'A bit on and off,' I said. Actually more off than on.

'What would you like to learn?' she asked.

'Well, I always wanted to jump,' I said, recalling my much-cherished hopeless fantasy of winning Olympia.

'Hmm. I think we'll start with walking first,' she said.

She reminded me of the aids to get a pony walking and Charlie and I set off around the arena. Charlie seemed willing enough in the way of small, forward-going ponies. I listened to the creak of the saddle as it moved on his back in time with his footfalls, felt the leather reins in my hands, the tacky feel of saddle soap, the coarse hair of the mane, and smelt the warm, sweet smell of the moving animal beneath me. A connection with something outside myself was beginning.

I completed two circuits in different directions and then the instructions started to flood in.

Stretch your lower legs down and push your heels down –
keep the ball of your foot on the stirrup – sit in the centre of the
saddle and look up between his ears – bend your elbows and turn
your wrists up – look in the direction you're going – squeeze the
rein – how do you expect him to know where to go if you're not
telling him?

And so on.

It came as a bit of a shock. From having escaped from my
body during the assault, I was now being told to be in it again
and to do things with it. It was involving a whole new rethink.
Where exactly were those heels I was supposed to be pushing
down? Which was right and left? How do you stop your head
from looking down or away when that's habitually how you look
at the world? In my autistic world, I lived internally, usually in a
mental space, and I had typically poor proprioception. Walking
round on a horse, it suddenly occurred to me just how much
time I spent in my head to the exclusion of all else.

But not only was I having to think in terms of my physical
self and of spatial awareness as I mapped out the various
dressage letters that are typically used around a riding-school
arena; I was now being given responsibility for guiding another
living creature around (although as a seasoned riding-school
pony Charlie could have done it blindfolded), for getting
him accurately around and across the school from B to E or
diagonally from K to M. This meant having to try to understand
things from a horse's perspective, appreciating the space a
horse needs to make a turn, guiding his vision in the direction I
wanted him to go – the theory of mind that people with autism
find so difficult.

When I'd mastered negotiating the arena (after a fashion), I
was asked if I wanted to trot. I hadn't ridden for years and, to be

quite honest, the thought sounded a bit scary (quite what I was expecting to happen I don't know) but I thought, having come this far, I might as well try it.

'Tell me the aids for trotting,' the instructor shouted at me.

'Er, kick a bit?' I hazarded.

'Wrong. We don't kick; we squeeze. Shorten your reins and prepare to go forward into trot.'

It took several squeezes for me to convince Charlie that 'go forward' meant 'go forward a bit faster'.

'Use your calves not your heels!' I was certainly getting a lesson in human anatomy today. Suddenly, Charlie lurched forward (in fact, he was just going into a trot) and I felt myself pitched in front of the saddle. I landed back into it with a bounce.

'Rise with the movement. Don't bounce on his back. I thought you said you'd ridden before.'

I would have told her that it was more than five years ago, but all my concentration was required now that Charlie was trotting. I rose stiffly up and down before falling into some sort of rhythm with him. Suddenly we hit a stride together.

'Well done.' That was my first bit of praise. 'Shorten your reins and prepare to walk.' We lurched to a stop. I'd overdone the braking.

'That'll do you for today,' she shouted. 'Not bad for a first go.'

I walked Charlie round the arena on a loose rein to cool him off (though he had hardly raised a sweat) and reluctantly dismounted.

Something remarkable had happened. I could not say exactly what, but I knew that the time I had spent on Charlie had been totally different to how time normally was for me at that point. Every swirling but unidentified negative feeling, all the fear, anxiety, guilt, remorse, rage and hurt had been forgotten in the process of learning to be with another sentient creature. I had moved from being, in a sense, outside of myself and detached from time and space to being wholly and fully in the present moment during the time that I had been with him. And I had wanted to be there.

I didn't want to get off him, either. On the ground I missed the sense of connection to something that I had felt whilst on his back. The four-time rhythmic beat of a horse in walk is like a rocking motion, a regular lulling pace that carries you along, soothing, taking away the stress. It wasn't something that could have been achieved by an inanimate machine, nor was it the traumatised rocking I had experienced at the hospital on the night of the attack (though I was probably unknowingly trying to achieve a similar effect at that time). I was sharing it with another living being in the most natural, non-demanding way: the horse was asking nothing back of me but was willing to let me share his space, his movement, his living, breathing presence.

I drove back home in a very different state from the one I had been in driving there. I was lighter, freer, connected back up to something. I didn't understand why – and if asked at the time, I wouldn't have been able to explain it – but one thing was certain: I was going back for more.

When the effect of that first riding experience had worn off, shortly after I returned home, I found myself questioning if it had really happened. I couldn't understand why I should have gone from the tortured place I had been in, the horrible stasis of a traumatised state, to a sense of wholeness and connectedness just by being with a horse. Following my logical brain, I put it down as a fluke, a strange one-off, and as the effects of the assault inexorably closed in on me and I reverted to what had become my usual frozen, paranoid state, I convinced myself that it was nothing more.

But I still wanted to go back and ride again, which in itself was a good sign, an indicator that I had found the self-motivation to at least do something. In those days when I needed an extremely good reason just to go out of the house, the fact that I was doing so voluntarily was a major achievement in itself. And so I duly went back and rode Charlie again. I came away the next time with the same sensation, only this time it lasted longer and felt even better. For one precious hour a week I had miraculously found a place where I could feel safe and whole and connected, a sanctuary in an otherwise unmitigated state of hopelessness. Very slowly something was beginning to shift in me.

Outside of the time spent with horses, my situation was as horrible as ever. I was still hardly eating and it was becoming more apparent. My collar bones were starting to stick out and my ribs were becoming visible. I remained detached from it all – I didn't want anything to do with my body, which still looked like a battleground. The bruises were slightly fainter and beginning to turn colour many weeks on from the assault, but the knife scars were just as visible. As far as I was concerned, my physical self no longer belonged to me anyway; my body was no longer *me* but an undefined *it*. Someone else had invaded *it* and driven me out, and I wanted nothing to do with *it* any more. I dressed and undressed in the dark to avoid looking at *it*; I didn't notice when *it* felt hungry or cold or tired.

In the scheme of things, I had got off reasonably lightly on the injury scale. Probably everything would heal in time, but what I felt would never heal was the sensation I now lived with of having looked at what I thought was going to be my own murder in the face, a moment of complete and utter powerlessness where all decisions are taken away and you can only look on helpless as fate takes its course. In that moment you are forced to recognise your own mortality; all the delusions you have shored up against your ruin – a sense of power, control, self-determination, choice, a future – crumble. You are in the truest sense powerless.

The few people whom I saw at the time commented on my lack of appetite and increasing thinness; they did their best to try to get me to eat but I couldn't. I had become locked in the fight-or-flight mechanism, where the activation of the sympathetic nervous system inhibits the digestive system. It was keeping me in a state in which I was permanently poised for flight. The threat was in the past, but, because of the traumatic response, I was still living as if it were real and present and liable to come back at any time. So I lived on the periphery of myself, ready to abscond at any moment.

Only when I was around horses did I seem to be able to be in myself and be in a fully present reality. Then I could not have explained it, but now, when I have had the chance to be around and observe horses and to learn about their behaviour over a number of years, I think I know why they had that effect on me. There were some similarities between the way I was experiencing the world then and the way horses do all the time: the horse is an herbivorous prey animal which has evolved over millennia to remain constantly vigilant and be prepared to flee from the threat of predators. Predators of the sabre-toothed-tiger variety might be rare in the Yorkshire Dales, but the instinct remains. Essentially, a horse always has the potential to flee, and the last thing a horse in flight mode needs is to be slowed down by too much hay in its belly. In a state of fear, at the moment at which it is poised for flight, a horse will not be able to eat. In my traumatised world, I had come to live in this state of endless fear of potential threat. Being around horses felt like being around a species which understood this state intimately and, on some instinctive level, I could feel this.

Another significant fact about horses, which I did not realise at the time, was that horses deal with the ever-present threat of predators by naturally living in herds, where herd members are always watchful for impending threats. It often falls to the herd stallion or alpha mare to do this in the wild, but all members remain vigilant to some degree (this is one reason why horses sleep standing up most of the time), so the task is shared and the stress and responsibility reduced. Hence horses feel much safer in a herd than they do alone.

I also found myself feeling much safer with horses than I did alone. Whereas being around humans remained a potentially stressful and overloading experience, being around horses did not. It was as if, for that brief hour a week, I could momentarily let go of my state of hyper-vigilance and borrow their watchfulness from them. Just being around them, I felt safer and calmer, much as I did with dogs, but with horses it seemed to enter a whole new dimension in which I seemed to enter and become a protected member of the herd.

Perhaps the most remarkable thing in all this was that I was gaining these benefits from just the brief period each week that I spent around horses in a man-made environment. At that point in my relationship with horses, I had no concept of how far the sense of connection and acceptance into the herd would eventually take me.

13

reaching out

I was, as always, spending the majority of my time alone, seeing no one but the dogs. I was used to this and preferred it normally, but I was not living in normal times: something inside me wanted to reach out and touch the human world again, if only for a brief spell. I had never been a total hermit, although I could get by practically on thin air in terms of human contact compared with most people. But the effects of isolation can be depleting, leading to a sense of emptiness and pointlessness, and I could only truly appreciate my inner world if I spent some time in the outer world – even if it was only for long enough to remind me why I disliked it so much. Work had fulfilled that role for me, forcing me into human contact whilst giving me the built-in boundary that people call Home Time. I did not miss working, but I did feel a need to connect again.

The Probation Service had decided that, in light of the poor response from their initial counselling service approach, they would fund me to see someone of my own choosing. It was up to me to find them. I had a lot of ambivalence about counselling and psychotherapy, partly from poor experiences in the past and partly because, being on the autistic spectrum, I wasn't a very likely candidate for it anyway. There were several issues from the autistic perspective: I disliked talking, especially about myself (I almost never disclosed personal information), I found it very difficult to identify what I was feeling beyond *OK* or *not OK*, and I had no ultimate expectation of graduating into a successful relationship/family/career – past therapists had always seemed to start with the premise that once I managed to form successful relationships I would become happy and fulfilled, whereas I was always aware on some level that this was never going to be a realistic option for me. And, apart from all that, sitting in a room being stared at by a stranger asking me how I felt and observing my every movement sounded like autistic hell.

There were other reasons too, which had more to do with my own cussedness. Being alone a lot and therefore rather let off the hook of social conventions and mores, I tended to give short shrift if I felt something was limited or faked for effect. Listening to people come out with trite phrases like 'I hear what you say' or 'Thank you for sharing that' riled me. And having what I'd said fed back to me nearly verbatim as a way of showing that someone was listening was thoroughly irritating.

In brief, I was not a good candidate for counselling or psychotherapy, and small wonder that in the past several had written me off or I had written them off.

But I was living in interesting times. My immediate problem was not how to live in a world where I didn't belong, but how to live in a world from which I'd been sent viciously flying. If anything could help me get back to *my* version of normality (and I was not optimistic), I was prepared to give it a go. So long, that is, as I didn't need to talk about my inner self or history or why I found it so difficult being around people.

As luck would have it, I had already met a potential counsellor whom I liked and trusted. Andy had worked for the Probation Service but also ran a private practice. In a roundabout way, it was thanks to Andy that I had got Poppy and Dessie with me now.

I'd been to see him once before on the advice of my manager, in connection with some difficult decisions I had to make about the possibility of working fewer hours (I was always hoping to do that). I met him in the neutral environment of his home near Bradford. Getting there had been a challenge. I had only been in Yorkshire for a short time and was still struggling to piece together the massive urban conurbation areas of Leeds and Bradford. As someone with Asperger's, I liked things to be clear-cut and logical, or at least to be able to assess and solve situations quickly and easily. There didn't seem to be anything clear-cut and logical about the drive through Bradford that evening. I drove through densely populated immigrant areas, something which still surprised me after Oxford and London where people seemed to integrate more. The few Asian men I stopped to ask the way were unable to help. I drove on, thinking that if I ever again saw signs telling me where I was headed, I would just drive straight home. When I had taken the most complicated route I possibly could through Bradford and out on the other side, I saw the road I needed to go on to get to Andy's house. It would have taken me 15 minutes if I'd driven from where I now lived. That's just one reason I came to prefer fields to cities.

I had come to the counselling session ostensibly to talk about work, but in a short while the real problem started to emerge. I'd moved to Yorkshire, having outlived the transient unreality of Oxford, because I had wanted a new start, a new challenge, and I'd got that. The other reason I'd moved was because of Ollie, my young Dalmatian. I'd needed a house with a big garden and more walking space to vent his inexhaustible energy, and this was never going to be affordable in Oxford. He was going to go to Yorkshire with me to run free on the Pennine moorland. But he had been killed three weeks before I moved. It was nearly a year ago now, but I was in tears as I described him to Andy.

After Minder, Ollie was my second dog and the first I had had from being a puppy. He was a strikingly handsome liver-spotted Dalmatian, so handsome that people would pull up in their cars to admire him. He was also the Hound from Hell whom no amount of training would ever tame. It's not that he didn't learn and learn quickly – I took him to numerous dog-training classes and he always outshone the other dogs – but he would only do it on his terms and when he wanted to (in that respect, I have to admit, he was a bit like me). They say you don't train a Dalmatian, you bribe them: come, sit, down, heel, fetch, stay, walk to heel and all the rest were easy-peasy as long as there was a piece of sausage at the end of it. If there wasn't, he would drag me down the road with incredible power, hell-bent on a walk; he howled for attention; he chewed well beyond the age when most puppies have stopped and he chewed on the grand scale. After sofa number four, I gave up – we could both sit on the floor for all I cared. Once I took him to stay with a dog-sitter for the day. I came back to find him banished to the kitchen behind a metal gate.

'Have you ever used him as a stud dog?' the dog-sitter asked me. I shook my head. 'It's just that he's very persistent with the other dogs. I've had to separate them.'

We both left with our tails between our legs.

It seemed we were always in some sort of trouble due to him jumping up, chasing things, going after other dogs. My self-imposed isolation was invariably broken by other dog owners' complaints and it used to infuriate me when people suggested I take him to training classes. I'd been taking him to training classes twice a week since he'd been 12 weeks old.

If things weren't going too well on the obedience side, Ollie was at least doing quite well as a potential show dog. He was handsome and had good breeding, and at his first show he qualified for Crufts. I took him to Crufts, that ultimate showcase of the nation's dog world, and he was placed third in his class. As a newcomer to showing, I was pleased to have done this well. A few weeks after Crufts, Ollie was killed.

I used to walk him on a large country park near Oxford, Boars Hill. It was fabulous walking territory with endless paths through woods and fields and hills. There was no reason for him to stray away: he could have walked for miles and miles without going near the busy by-pass at the edge of the park.

When I first noticed that he was missing, I didn't worry. As a big active dog, he could range far and sausages normally worked for a recall if nothing else. But this time I called and called for him, waiting to see his spotty muzzle emerge through the ferns and long grass. Even though he was naughty, he would always come back eventually – after all, breakfast came after a walk and in Ollie's scheme of things that was the next best thing. After three hours of searching, I had no choice but to report him missing to the police and return home. It was a ghastly feeling – Ollie might be a nightmare at times, but in my autistic world he was all I had. Most of all, I feared that if he had been stolen, I would never know if he was all right, if he was safe and warm and looked after.

The police call came in the afternoon. The policeman, who broke it to me as gently as he could, said Ollie had strayed on to the by-pass and been run over. He had been identified by the tag on his collar.

'Where is he now?' I asked, my voice low and husky.

'He's still next to the by-pass. We'll arrange for him to be removed.'

'I'll go up and see him.' My voice was still low and toneless.

He tried to dissuade me: 'It might be better to remember him as he was.' Perhaps he was trying to protect me from looking at crushed and mutilated remains. I didn't care. I wanted to see him. I took the location details and went straight to the car.

On the way up I was crying uncontrollably. The most important thing in the world, in *my* world, had gone. I parked up the car in a layby on the by-pass and found him lying stiff by the side of the road. The only sign of injury was a trickle of blood running from his brown-button dog nose – maybe he had been hit on the skull by a car. There were no other broken bones or cuts, and he lay as beautiful in death as he had been alive; only his irrepressible Dalmatian spirit had gone. I knelt beside him and began retching with grief as if something was being torn out of me. I laid my head on his stiffening side and knew that now there would be no future together in Yorkshire or anywhere else. I angrily brushed away a fly that had dared to land on his head, his beautiful, spotty head with its soft ears and brown eyes that were now glazed and half shut.

When a car pulled up next to us with a lady and her teenage son in it, I dragged my attention away from Ollie. The son wound down the window and looked at me, uncertain what to say.

'Are you all right?' the woman asked. 'Is there anything you need?' I was surprised. Oxford wasn't the sort of place where strangers asked if you were all right. People kept themselves to themselves.

'I'm all right, thank you,' I mumbled, despite overwhelming evidence to the contrary. She looked askance at me. 'My dog's been killed.' I indicated Ollie and they both looked down.

'Oh, I'm so sorry. Are you sure there's nothing we can do? Can we give you a lift anywhere?'

'No, thank you. I'm going soon.' When they had gone, I gave Ollie the last kiss I would ever give him and walked back to the car, stiff from kneeling so long. A police car had pulled up next to it. A large policeman got out and walked towards me.

'Can I ask what you've been doing?' he asked, not unkindly.

'My dog's been killed,' I said, jerking one hand in the direction where Ollie lay and brushing away tears with the other one. His face fell and a look of pity spread over it.

'Oh, I'm really sorry to hear that. A lorry driver rang us to say there was an empty car and someone sitting next to the by-pass.'

Probably they thought I was going to do a suicide run. Again I was surprised by the kindness of strangers. It seemed that it was always in my moments of desperation that someone actually bothered about me. The policeman said some more kind words to me, and he and his colleague saw me safely on to the by-pass to drive away. The back seat was empty without Ollie.

That night I had the strangest dream I have ever had. I dreamed of Ollie, but it was as if I were inside him, as if I were in fact Ollie, experiencing the world through a dog's consciousness, through the scent and hearing and sight of a dog. *We* were walking through grass on all fours. It reached up to nose level; *we* could smell it very strongly. *We* were curiously carefree in a way that humans usually aren't; it was a being-in-the-moment sensation where neither the past nor the future mattered. *We* walked easily under a wooden barrier when something hit *us* and there was almost instant oblivion.

Whether that is how it happened to Ollie, I will never know. But I never afterwards worried that he had felt frightened or suffered before he died. In my dream of Ollie I may have come closer to understanding the animal world, however briefly.

Andy listened patiently, and if he thought I was bonkers to still be crying for a dog that had died a year ago, he didn't show it. He seemed to understand when I explained about my need to be alone a lot of the time, how I had always felt more comfortable around animals than humans and how alone I felt now that Ollie was gone.

Then he asked the question. 'Why don't you get another dog?'

I could think of a lot of reasons. Living alone and being at work meant leaving the dog home alone, not something I wanted to do, especially with a young puppy.

'They do learn to cope,' he said. 'All ours have managed, and if it means having something in your life that you love, you could get someone to come in and walk it. And you could always get two dogs so they're not alone. I seem to remember that some people used to take their dogs into work too.'

It sowed a thought in me and the thought kept growing. The upshot was that I got Poppy: another liver Dalmatian came into my life. She was the exact opposite of Ollie; it was hard to believe they were the same breed. Poppy was loyal, trainable, loving, easy to please and very placid. When Poppy was eight months old, Dessie joined us. Dessie was a black-spotted Dalmatian, small from having come from a litter of 16 puppies and so beautiful she would always take my breath away whenever I looked at her. She seemed to have been born with an inbuilt assumption that the world was put there solely for the purpose of her to love it and for it to love her. For the most part, the 'world' that she knew took her at her own assumption. Beautiful, coy, sex-kittenish (if you can say that about a dog), she charmed everyone she came into contact with and she loved me more than anything in the whole wide loving world she lived in. Most of all she loved physical closeness. She would follow me everywhere, sit patiently for hours when I was reading, eventually pushing the book out of my hand if she thought she was due for some attention and climbing on to my knee. She also had a way of putting her front legs around your arm or neck as if she was giving you a hug in human terms; she was endlessly tactile, constantly wanting to bury her head against you as if she was trying to enter your very being. She was my dog of a lifetime.

In large measure it was thanks to Andy that I got the dogs when I did and that they were there for me, as nothing else was, when the assault happened.

Ringing Andy's number from my traumatised world was a major effort. I never felt comfortable reaching out into the outer world, and the fact that I was in effect going to be asking someone to help me felt awkward, strange, almost humiliating. And, apart from that, I was haunted by a sneaking suspicion that on some level I deserved what I had got, that I did not deserve to heal from what had happened because somehow it was all my fault anyway.

After a considerable amount of inner debate I dialled his number one evening. A woman answered the phone.

'Can I speak to Andy, please?'

'Who is this?' Her tone sounded strange, almost shrill.

I reluctantly explained who I was and why I was ringing. I heard something that sounded like a sob.

'Andy passed away,' she said, a tremor in her voice. 'He died three weeks ago.' She broke down in tears.

'I'm so sorry,' I said, shocked and stunned.

She told me he had died of a heart attack. I listened and wondered what to say. 'He was very kind to me when I saw him,' I said. 'It made a big difference to me.' I didn't explain just how big a difference having the dogs had made. I told her to take care of herself and she told me to do the same, adding, 'I hope you get the help you need.'

I put the phone down and stared at the wall for a long time. A mixture of feelings was brewing up inside me. I felt bad, guilty for having intruded on someone else's grief, stupid for bringing my own petty concerns at a time like that. But also I felt myself cursed – in an irrational way I felt that I had become some sort of harbinger of death, a cursed person who seemed to curse whoever I came into contact with, someone who should stay away from other people. Lastly I felt sickened and angry at what seemed to be yet another sick joke that the universe was playing on me.

Andy's death played into a wider pervasive sense of guilt that haunted me at the time. I felt guilty on several levels: guilt for having precipitated this mess in the first place, guilt about M's death, guilt for having involved a colleague in an assault that had been fundamentally aimed at me. And whilst no one appeared to be blaming me, no one actually said I was innocent either. Being as isolated as I was, no one contradicted the self-accusations that I occasionally openly levelled at myself or which constantly haunted the peripheries of my thinking.

My aloneness, my sense of being a permanent outsider, compounded the situation. Not only had the assault effectively removed me from contact with the wider world, it had left me to face the sense I always had that I was at best a tolerated outsider in it, a refugee in a foreign country. And, as an outsider, your rights are fewer, your sense of entitlement reduced. If you make a mistake as an outsider, where is the forgiveness? I expected none and gave myself none.

The emotions of post-traumatic stress segued continuously. It was a complicated picture in which I could be victim and accused, fugitive and fighter, guilty and not guilty. In this maelstrom, animals provided a consistent, calming force, the still eye of the storm, unchanging, silent and accepting. Animals do not blame – it is one of their many graces. Poppy and Dessie's acceptance of me was without condition, never wavering, questioning or looking askance. The horses I rode every week did not care what had happened yesterday or what would happen tomorrow. They existed wholly in the present and, for the time I was with them, so did I – free of guilt. They provided me with a grounding source, a sensory reality, a presence which required that I focus outside of myself sometimes and in so doing connect with another reality.

Eventually I did find a counsellor I could talk to about the events of the assault. Her name was Vicky and she had had extensive experience in trauma counselling. Each week I talked endlessly about the event, the circumstances around it, my feelings of guilt. She listened patiently. She didn't blame me; she explained about survivor guilt, the process whereby survivors of a traumatic event can blame themselves for various aspects of it – causing it, failing to prevent it, surviving it. I learned about the frequently irrational thought processes that go on after a traumatic event. The after-effects remained the same, but I began slowly to feel differently about them, to begin to consider them in slightly different ways. I still blamed myself and I would do so for a very long time to come (even today I am not totally free of guilt), but I knew now that there was one other person out there apart from the animals who didn't. I was grateful to Vicky.

14

post-traumatic stress

I had been riding for several weeks now and it was by far the best time in the week. When I was around horses, I felt all right – no, not just all right, actually inside myself and at peace. It seemed miraculous that, when things had seemed so ruined, I could go from that cold, alien, dissociated state, where everything felt lost and irrecoverable, to a state that felt the exact opposite. I think that just being around horses had an amazing effect in itself – sitting on a horse and feeling that comforting, rocking motion, having a short time of connection with another live, warm being who did not threaten me or judge me or ask anything of me other than to be still with him was reaping huge benefits in itself.

But the focus at that time was essentially on learning to ride and it was the act of learning to ride that really stretched me and helped me move on from my stuck place. I had not told anyone at the riding school about my experience of the assault, so no one was treating me with kid gloves, and riding instructors, historically anyway, are not known for calling a spade an implement to dig with. Once sitting on a horse, a barrage of challenging questions would bring me up short as I was going round the arena.

'*Do you normally look the other way when you go round a corner?*'

'*Would you be walking on tiptoes if you were walking down the street? Get your heels down!*'

'*Why would you be looking down when you're trying to get somewhere?*' (Actually, in my case that would depend on whether someone else was coming towards me. I was adept at blocking out people in crowded spaces where the sensory overload could overwhelm me.)

'*If you were driving a car, would you be using the accelerator and the brakes at the same time? I'm glad I'm not in your passenger seat.*'

'*Bring your elbows in. You look like a duck.*'

And so on. Above all activities, horse riding forces us to rethink our body, its movements and its effects. The smallest motion of the head, a change of direction of the eyes, a shift in body weight can all lead to a different response from the horse. I would later learn that even a change of thought can do it too, though I wouldn't have believed it at the time, not having begun to fathom the depths of a horse's sensitivity. To be a good rider requires extremely subtle alterations and an acute awareness of what we are doing physically. I was a million miles away from being even a mediocre rider, but I was learning to piece together parts of myself, to learn new movements, new responses, and to do this and because I wanted to learn, I had to be inside myself again.

Being inside myself, for the duration of the ride, had other effects apart from reconnecting me. For most of my life I had lived internally and done my best to keep the outer world at bay. Prior to the assault I had read and thought incessantly, and whilst part of me enjoyed this process for its own sake and revelled in the endless possibilities of thought and knowledge, another part of me used the process to block out the outside social world in all its engulfing and overwhelming mess. The result was that I tended to be unbalanced – very heavily weighted towards the thinking inner world and fairly incompetent at dealing with the mundane reality in front of me. When I was riding, it seemed my right hand had to literally know what my left hand was doing – the consequences could be a horse wandering off with you on top of it. By being around horses, having to be there in the present, dealing with a practical reality that involved another sentient being, I was beginning in a small way to start to address some of the imbalance. I was never going to be the most practical, connected person in the world, but perhaps I could learn to stay connected to the present reality a little bit more.

To add to this already impressive suite of benefits, there is another one: riding a horse means being in control, or at least that is the theory. The moment of the assault had reduced me to a sense of utter powerlessness – a sense that someone else was taking the decision about whether to let me live or die. Although I was still alive, I could no longer take that state for granted, no longer assume that my life was under my control. But you cannot take responsibility for another creature when you are powerless.

At the riding school I had graduated from 13-hands Charlie to bigger mounts. Ginny, at 17 hands and built like a carthorse, was no lightweight to control and neither was Mac, a 16.2 Irish Draught former hunter. For the time I was riding it was up to me to assume control over these giants: where they went, what speed they went at, when they stopped and when they started. And if I didn't assume control, there were consequences. A horse is not an inanimate machine – it is not fooled by humans who don't know what they are doing or who pretend to be in charge when they are not. I had to reassume a sense of power and control if I was to stand a chance of getting the horse to work with me – a literal and metaphorical taking back the reins. And whilst I would in the following years learn that riding is much more an art of cooperation than control, being put back in a position of control during that time of post-traumatic stress restored to me some of the empowerment that I had lost during the assault.

There were carry-over effects too. The art of riding had intrigued me and, as always when intrigued, I wanted to find out more. I started to read about it, which meant I was beginning to engage with something again. I know now that you cannot learn horsemanship from a book, even though I had learned so many things that way: horsemanship requires a real, hands-on presence and not only a physical presence but an intuitive, sensitive response and an ability to communicate that transcends words. But for then it was a start just to find out more and it led me to think in odd moments about physical reactions and the effect they would have on the horse – a clenched fist on the rein, for example, would send one sort of message, an unclenched fist another and so on. On some level I was thinking inside myself again.

But I was still a long way off recovery.

I was crouching in the corner of the shop, willing myself to disappear into the magnolia-coloured wall in front of me. I wanted to stay perfectly still, but my hands were shaking and my teeth were chattering.

He was standing somewhere at my back. I had seen *him* in the queue in front of me, recognised the blue tinge of his shaven head, the same powerful build, the broad shoulders and the arms with their preternatural strength.

I pressed my forehead against the wall. If I stayed here, he might, just might, not see me. I waited, blocking out everything around me.

'Art tha reet, lass?' A voice to the side of me spoke in broad Yorkshire. An older man in a flat cap and glasses was looking down on me. I half glanced at him and turned back to the wall.

'Yes, I'm all right, thanks.'

'Are you poorly?'

I shook my head and risked another half glance to the side of me. A mirror on the wall looked across at a mirror behind the counter. According to the mirrors, the queue had disappeared. *He* had gone.

I stood up and slowly turned around.

'Just felt a bit sick,' I muttered to the man and the shop assistant behind the counter. 'I'm OK now.'

'Aye, it's 'er prices in 'ere.' He gave a mock grin in the direction of the woman behind the counter. 'It's enough to make anybody sick.'

'You keep coming back, though,' she retorted.

'It's the pleasure of your company.'

I scanned the shop. *He* was nowhere to be seen. My car was outside (I never walked anywhere I didn't have to these days).

'Thanks,' I said again and left the shop without buying anything. Keeping my head down and my peripheral vision blocked, I walked through a tunnel to the car. Somewhere behind me I heard a woman's voice: 'She were a bit strange.'

'Proper weird,' added another.

'Nowt as queer as folk,' said the man who had spoken to me.

I saw my dead attacker often in those days. He was out there in the streets, and he was still intent on killing me. No amount of rationalisation or logical consideration could override that part of my brain which knew he was still alive and still a threat. Any unfortunate man of a certain height with a shaven head was a potential suspect.

That was in life. In my dreams he was still there too, with his hideous face, his freaky, quiet, gentle voice issuing the same threat, his powerful ham fist clenching the bread knife from my own kitchen. In dreams he was not alive but a visitor from some underworld, a Hades for the damned. His mother still haunted my dreams too, reminding me whose fault it was that he had died, reminding me that there is no forgiveness for murderers.

Sometime later, when I discovered the actual circumstances following his death, I found the reality more chilling. I learned that his mother had wanted nothing to do with him, that only a drunken uncle had turned up for the funeral. There were no other friends or relations.

I was sitting in another doctor's waiting room, this time at the West Yorkshire Police headquarters near Wakefield. I was waiting to be seen by a police doctor having been referred for an assessment by the occupational health department of the Probation Service, and I was shaking. The drive had been traumatic: I had had to drive on part of the route I would normally have taken to get to work, to get to the place where *it* happened, a journey I had not made since *it* happened. My heart had begun to beat faster as I came into proximity. In spite of the road cameras, I put my foot down, accelerating out of the area as fast as possible.

It had taken me over an hour to drive there and after so long at home I was definitely out of my comfort zone. Now, in the waiting room at the Police headquarters, my heart was still beating madly. An off-duty (possibly on-sick) young policeman joined me. He started chatting in an easy comradely fashion, perhaps assuming I was part of the police force. I wondered what horrors the police were exposed to in the line of duty, although it turned out that this young policeman had strained his ankle during a training session.

I was called through. A bearded doctor with glasses shook my hand and invited me to sit down and tell him what had happened. He had already read a report so I outlined the bare details, not really wanting to talk about it anyway.

He nodded. 'Sounds pretty nasty. How does it affect you now?'

I gave him a litany of the dreary symptoms: not eating, nightmares, sleeping too much, fear of going outside, fear of people, fear of seeing him in the streets, no longer feeling inside myself, everything in ruins… I didn't mention that I felt guilty over it as well: I felt too ashamed.

'Are you on edge a lot?' I nodded. 'Feel angry sometimes?' I nodded.

'Post-traumatic stress,' the doctor pronounced. 'I'd be very surprised if you weren't suffering from it after something like that, where you felt your life was under threat. The main thing is to try to stop it becoming too entrenched. What help have you had so far?'

I told him I had just started counselling and mentioned that my GP had prescribed Prozac (I didn't mention the horse riding as I didn't think it would fit into any particular medical model). He grimaced slightly at the word 'counselling'.

'Counselling's all right in its way, but it's not guaranteed to work in cases like this. It sometimes keeps you stuck in reliving things. There's a treatment for post-traumatic stress called EMDR. Heard of it?'

Maybe it was a rhetorical question.

'It stands for Eye Movement Desensitisation and Reprocessing,' he said and went on to explain it. Briefly, EMDR was developed by an American psychologist, Francine Shapiro, in the late 1980s. The aim of EMDR is to allow individuals experiencing unprocessed trauma to process stuck, distressing memories and hence move on from the trauma. As the name suggests, it is done in part by recounting the distressing memories whilst moving the eyes from side to side.

Being slightly miffed at his response to counselling (if only out of loyalty to Vicky), I was tempted to ask at what point in the proceedings do you rub a turnip around your head, but I refrained. Then again, if I'd mentioned the horse riding, he could have asked me which particular shaman I'd got that from. Perhaps none of it really matters as long as you find something that works.

'It sounds a bit strange,' was all I said. He agreed and went on to demonstrate the eye movement following a finger. He gave me several examples of where it had been used in the police force for police officers involved in shootings, sieges and stand-offs.

He seemed keen for me to try it. 'I'd like to refer you to a psychologist who does it, but I need to have your permission and that of the Probation Service.'

Without knowing quite what I was agreeing to, I said I would try it. I would have tried anything to get back to the normality I had once known, to the world where I didn't know then what I wish I didn't know now. The old world seemed like an Edenic place, and if in reality it had been anything but prelapsarian, at least I hadn't been scared to go outside my own front door. There weren't going to be any easy answers, I understood that much. Trauma by its very nature keeps you stuck and it can last years, even a lifetime. Sometimes it repeats itself endlessly and at others buries so deeply you cannot access it, but it continues to poison your life and will one day surely come out to meet you head on. And I wanted to be free of it.

The most relief I could hope for at that time was that which came from horses. I had ridden several different horses by now, but it didn't seem to matter: the transformative effect or what I came to call the *horse effect* was the same. For the time I was on them or with them, I felt whole and safe.

At about this time a strange thought was beginning to occur to me: *What if I could experience this every day with horses, not just once a week for an hour?*

Having grown up in a world where the question 'Can I have a horse?' invariably met with an instant 'No', I didn't take the thought of owning a horse too seriously. In all my experience, horses were for other people – people with money and land or people lucky enough to have parents who bought them for them, kids who grew up initiated into the mysteries of horse ownership from an early age. Not for me.

But the question was there: *What if?*

A horsebox load of questions and objections flocked willingly and predictably to mind: You don't get your first horse when you're approaching 40. Where would you keep it? You don't know how to look after it. It would cost too much and there's no money.

The last was a bit of a sore point. I had received a standardised letter from the Probation Service informing me that, due to my continued absence on sick leave, my pay would be reduced to half and in a further three months to nothing if I didn't come back. Knowing nothing about my rights or union law, I felt unduly pressurised into going back, back to the place of my assault. No one else was going to support me if I didn't.

Otherwise, I had heard nothing from my workplace or colleagues for weeks. I rang up on one occasion to try to clarify the situation about some money that was owed to me in expenses. I didn't want to because I assumed, going on the evidence of the silence, that no one wanted to speak to me for whatever reason. But my finances were being squeezed to the limit and every penny counted. Expecting a fairly indifferent response due to my prolonged absence and the continued silence, I rang up. I couldn't have been more wrong. Everyone wanted to talk to me. It came in a babble:

'We've talked about you non-stop, but we were told not to contact you.'

'Is there anything at all that you need or we can do for you?'

'Just take care of yourself and get better – no one is expecting you to rush back.'

I put the phone down, stunned. So I wasn't being ignored or sent to a form of Coventry. If I could have voiced my need for help in the early days, it sounded as if I would have got it, and whilst my autistic self would have been very unlikely to ask, it had actually transpired that no one was able to reach out and offer it to me. I wondered again why they had been told not to contact me when they were the very people who knew what had happened. Working around the clock in a residential setting, especially one where the clients can be difficult and dangerous, breeds a particular closeness amongst work colleagues, especially when you share a lot of time together during unsocial hours. It had given me a link to that other world which I had had to deal with, a connection, however tenuous, that was tolerable because it occupied a discrete time and place, with inbuilt boundaries. I had liked and respected the people I had worked with and I had felt myself banished by the assault. The enforced silence was baffling. Whatever the reason, it left a bitter taste in my mouth as I put the phone down.

15

facing demons

It was early summer and Wimbledon was in full swing. Inside the psychologist's office, I was getting my own particular version of tennis. A small object moved horizontally backwards and forwards across the computer screen, a bit like a very early computer game that mimicked ping-pong. My instructions were to follow it by moving my eyes backwards and forwards with it, whilst recounting the details of the assault in every detail possible.

I burst into nervous laughter. It felt a bit ridiculous.

'Sorry,' I apologised to the psychologist, expecting him to be annoyed with me, as if I'd laughed in church or at a funeral. 'I was just thinking about the semi-finals.'

'That's OK.' He wasn't annoyed. 'It happens a lot to people. Take as much time as you need.'

I watched the screen and recounted what had happened, guided by questions from the psychologist. I liked the psychologist – he was very down-to-earth, the kind of person I found easy to deal with because I didn't have to interpret the usual confusing battery of social signals. As well as the EMDR, he had also done some tests on my breathing, explaining that in traumatic situations breathing can become very shallow. Normally this is restored after the event; where the trauma is severe, however, it can persist, effectively keeping someone in a state of panic. Tests revealed that my breathing was abnormally shallow.

'Which side is fullest?' he had asked me.

'Sorry?'

'Your nose.'

'Oh, you mean...'

'Yes, which side has most snot in it?'

He told me to shut the side that was emptier and breathe through the more blocked-up one, encouraging very deep, slow breathing. He explained the benefits of this to me and sent me away to practise.

I had several sessions with him. I can't say for definite whether the EMDR had any effect or not, unlike the horse riding where I definitely felt immediate and tangible benefits when I was with the horse and for increasingly longer periods afterwards. Perhaps it is hard to tell when several different kinds of therapies (counselling, drugs, EMDR and horses) are going on at the same time, and maybe they were all working on some level. But I knew which one I preferred.

I remained in a state of hyper-vigilance, distanced from myself and everything around me, for some time to come. My inability to eat remained drearily the same, perhaps having by now mutated into an entrenched pattern. My memories of anorexia were burned into my brain and I knew how hard it is to go back to eating normally again once eating patterns are thoroughly disrupted. It looked as if it wasn't going to be any easier now. I had lost more than two stones and I found myself starting to obsess about food in the way that happens with prolonged hunger. Now I didn't just dash into a supermarket and dash out again in a bid to get home. I found myself looking at the food on the shelves for long periods, concocting recipes, desperately trying to recall the tastes. It was ironic for me to spend any time there because, in my previous (for that, read pre-assault) life, places like supermarkets – their crowds, arguing couples, screaming children and an invasive tannoy system – played hell with my sensory system. In my more misanthropic moments, I regarded supermarkets as the most compelling reason yet against human reproduction. Now I was more likely to become annoyed if someone walked between me and the bread shelves I was staring at, resenting the interruption to my fantasy about the smell and taste of newly baked bread. It was a look-but-don't-touch world, because I almost invariably returned home empty-handed. Why buy food when you know you won't eat it? I watched from the sidelines as my hips and ribs grew more prominent and my clothes began to hang off me. Months on from the assault, the mass of cuts and bruises that had turned me into a human artist's palette of browns and blues and purples and reds and greens and yellows earlier in the year had nearly gone, except for one particularly vicious and intractable bruise on my right thigh. Several scars across my chest and stomach were there to see if I cared to look. Mostly I didn't. I still didn't want to own my own body.

But, for all that, a part of me craved some sort of normality, a return to how things had been, if that were ever going to be possible. Being alone in the house all day was starting to send me up the four unspeaking walls. I was starting to crave some mental stimulus too, but I still couldn't read (a fact I resented more than anything else – reading had always been my salvation), and, much as I loved the dogs, conversation tended to be philosophically limited. I could try to enter Dessie's world by talking to her about the relative merits of Pedigree Chum and Chappie, or tell Poppy that it was considered bad form to dig up bones from the garden and bring them in the house, but this only went so far. Normality meant going back to work, picking up where I had left off. Except that work was also the scene of the assault. Moving on, getting back to 'normal', also meant facing demons.

I had been visited by my manager and a member of the human resource team in my own home. I had not wanted the visit, always having held to a personal rule that work and anything connected to it were entirely separate from my home life. Additionally, I had adapted to the quiet isolation of days spent at home alone. A visit, especially from those in a position of power, felt threatening and invasive, but I wasn't comfortable spending time outside the house either, so I gave in with bad grace, privately giving the dogs full licence to jump up and be a nuisance for the whole of the visit. When they came, I was glad to have Dessie snuggling up close to me, providing the only security I could envisage.

The lady from the human resource team looked at me curiously when she came into my house. I glared back, partly because it failed to respect one of my private autistic needs not to be stared at and partly because I was still liable to go on the defensive because of the assault. She looked away. I realised she had probably just been curious about me: the incident had sparked a lot of paperwork and talk across the Probation Service. I backed down a bit and went to sit on the sofa with Dessie.

They were as tactful as possible, making it clear that I was under no pressure to go back before I was ready, and that if I was unable to cope with working in the same environment, I would be transferred. I was also told that my wage would in fact remain unaltered during the time I was off sick (although in reality an administrative cock-up resulted in no payment for months, which created undue pressure for me to go back).

Several months on from the attack, I decided it was time to face my demons.

My pulse was racing as I pulled into the car park at work. A flood of memories was coming back to me, none of them pleasant. They rushed through my mind:

This is where…

And here's when…

And in there…

I couldn't finish any of them. I had only got this far by sheer willpower, a kind of holding my head down and running at it. To think too hard could be fatal. Still with my head down, poised for whatever was coming to me, I rang the entry buzzer. Several faces looked out at me from the office window. They were smiling, pleased to see me. My return visit was being carefully orchestrated to last no more than an hour.

The greeting inside the office was overwhelming. There were tears and hugs all round and, despite being the least touchy-feely person alive, I was swept up in it. I looked incredulously round the office, site of so many horrible and haunting memories which had been repeating themselves for months. I saw the corner by the wall where I had gone into a foetal curl, exited myself and waited to be killed, looked at the door *he* had ran through after threatening to kill me, saw the desk where my work colleague had taken a horrible beating...

Now I was seeing it in daylight, full of happy normal people.

'This is so weird,' I said, stuck for anything to say and overwhelmed by the buzz of activity after my months of solitude.

One thing everyone agreed on: 'You look different.'

It was John who guessed the reason correctly: 'Is it the crash diet, Sue?' Another colleague came in and gave me a hug before standing back in amazement: 'You're like a pencil. There's nothing there.'

After some small talk about Wimbledon and the World Cup, I was whisked away to the manager's office, on my way receiving another hug from Karen, the newly pregnant cleaner.

'It's lovely to see you back,' she said, adding, 'I've gained weight and you've lost it.'

'At least yours is in a good cause,' I smiled.

I spent some time in the manager's office. He was very kind to me and filled me in on what had happened after the assault, but I found some of it difficult to listen to. I was not ready to hear about the details of the death of my assailant – I had yet to fully process my own feelings about it, which continued to swing between guilt and anger and terror. I didn't quite realise until that moment of talking about the assault how fragile and vulnerable I still felt. It was strange – in my independent, self-sufficient world, these were luxuries (as I viewed them) which I could not afford to feel, designations that people might possibly make about you from without, but not ones which would ever come from within. It seemed strange too to be admitting that I wasn't ready to go beyond the office out to where the residents congregated. It was somewhere between a phobia and a stereotype. One very bad experience had left me wary of all offenders: all were a potential threat in a way I had never considered before. A few steps would have taken me to them, but today they were a step too far.

I was there for an hour and I had got over what was probably the worst part – going through the front door again. The rest could wait for now. I drove home and slept for a solid 15 hours afterwards.

Once I had made my initial visit, it seemed to be taken as read that I was going to be coming back to work. And I did return, slowly, gradually. At first it was for a few hours a week, then half a day and eventually a full day a week. But something had changed. I no longer felt comfortable spending time away from home: the only place I felt safe (with the exception of sitting on a horse) was behind my own locked front door. It was different from the usual need to retreat to my internal autistic world, which was mostly caused by sensory overload from being around other people. Now it was based purely on a kind of fear. I struggled to go into work in the morning, inventing endless excuses and rituals to defer the departure. When I returned home, I only wanted to sleep and would do so for hours and hours at a time.

Looking back, I think I had felt unduly pressurised into returning to work and had gone back too soon. Financial worries and isolation had played a part in this, but so had a lack of any adequate guidance about what was the best thing to do when recovering (for I was now in that phase, if only the very early days) from post-traumatic stress. It was a journey into unknown territory which would only be discovered along the way.

The issue was further complicated by the fact that my workplace was also the place of the attack. People with post-traumatic stress disorder are sometimes encouraged to visit the scene of whatever it was that left them traumatised as a way of allaying the outsize demons that can take over if not measured against the current reality. One visit back might have sufficed, but I was eventually revisiting it every day. At first I had stayed well clear of the probation clients, refusing to go beyond the office or managerial area. I was quite simply afraid, unable to trust, wary of what lurked, even though it was now there to be seen in daylight with potentially five other people to support me. In fact, being able to talk to and intermingle with the residents again was a major part of the healing. I had to learn again that they weren't all monsters, that they didn't necessarily pose a threat to me, that they were fellow human beings. Through mingling with them, I came to see that actually, no matter what their criminal record, most people were not a direct threat to me. And if *they* were not a threat, who was?

In some ways the residents were one of the best things about my return. They all knew what had happened to me. Sometimes those who are marginalised or on the outside of society can have a very instinctive understanding of hurt and vulnerability because, let's face it, most of them end up where they do because they have been hurt, neglected, abused and marginalised. I was deeply touched by the sensitivity and caring they showed to me. They tried to make sure I ate at mealtimes (not very successfully, but the thought was there); they treated me as if they knew I was fragile and not fully operational. Several of them told me how sorry they were about what had happened (usually it was followed by something like 'I'll kill that fucker if I ever come across him', unaware that 'that fucker' was already dead). One told me: 'I know what it's like. I got stabbed once and it takes ages to get over it. I really think you've got bottle coming back here.'

But my 'bottle' was distinctly challenged. My world view had been changed and I heard and saw things differently, always alert now to threats or potential threats. On my first full day back at work, several weeks after my initial visit, a client came into the office shouting at a member of staff. *Before*, it would not have bothered me, but now was *after* and I found myself retreating away into the staff room, unable to cope. Other incidents inevitably occurred and were reported back amongst the staff, many involving threats or potential threats. It was in the nature of the place, and I quickly saw that it was the wrong place for me to be.

During my phased return to work I had not been on night duty which would have involved working alone. I don't think anyone ever seriously thought I would go back to it again – certainly I knew it would be impossible for me. Most of my colleagues were highly supportive, but the Probation Service itself, in the nature of public service organisations, hidebound by bureaucratic procedures and protocol and people in senseless jobs creating even more senseless rulings, was not. It filtered down to me that unless I went back to my old job, recognised by everyone who knew what had happened to me as not viable, I could either move to one on a comparable scale (none existed as hostel work was fairly distinct from field and prison work) or find another job somewhere else.

I felt deeply angry. Maybe I was also starting to question and feel angry about what had happened to me. Others had expressed disgust about it, but to date I had largely blamed myself, guilt and self-recrimination preventing me from looking at the wider picture. Now, however, I started to question why I had been put in such a vulnerable position in the first place. Why had two women been left in sole charge of a hostel of 20 highly dangerous offenders with limited night-time back-up? Why were people about whom relatively little was really known being released from prison prior to the weekend when only a limited number of staff were about? Why were the hostels being forced into taking people who were not suitable for release from the prisons because the prisons were at breaking point? Why were dangerous prisoners released early simply on the basis that they said the right thing to get out? Why had my life and that of a colleague been so damaged because of a system that had failed to deliver what was needed?

All of this and the feeling that I was now being put in a position where I would lose my job made me furious. The situation reached deadlock: I wasn't going anywhere; I wasn't going to quietly walk away after going through all that. I felt something at least was owed to me. The service wasn't moving on the position because it was too tied up in bureaucracy to find a flexible or creative solution. In the meantime, I remained in limbo, turning up for work during the day, not really having any work to do, whilst constantly remaining exposed to reminders and threats of potential violence.

One morning I had simply had more than I could take of this exposure. After listening to a graphically imagined description of what could potentially happen if a resident turned violent, a report of another resident who had come into the office and told staff what he would do to them if he wasn't allowed home leave this weekend, and listening to residents joking about which was the best knife blade on the market, I announced that I was leaving.

I drove home with a racing heart. On the way I stopped by the roadside and retched violently into the hedgerow.

I stayed away for several weeks, furious about everything. I was back where I had started in terms of achieving 'normality' and I had no idea what was going to happen and when. The uncertainty of this limbo state was the last thing I needed. My main memories of that time are of pounding across the moors with the dogs, cursing my situation and everyone connected with it. It was midsummer and the purple heather of the Yorkshire moors was coming out. The quality of the heather can be variable, with some years producing a much stronger purple than others. I remember the colour that summer, when I spent so much time on it, as being deep and glorious and spread out everywhere. As I pounded over the heather, walked through the ferns, over the mossy boulders and the big granite rocks, I found myself wondering why I wanted to be connected with the criminal world in all its grim ugliness anyway? Surely it was time to start thinking about doing something a bit easier, something that would give me more time to spend with the dogs and horses which mattered far more to me?

At work I still wasn't going to just give in and walk away. A large amount of stubbornness born of a sense of righteous anger on my part, some union involvement and doubtless the threat of a court case on their hands forced the Probation Service to capitulate. In a laughable *volte face* which they claimed had been their intention all along, I was offered a better job with better pay, nine to five. At the age of 40 I had finally found a respectable job. I accepted it, glad that the situation had been resolved, but with the usual ambivalence that any job where I would have to interact with others brought out in me.

There was something else I wanted to do to prove to myself that things were returning to normal. A year previously I had planned to go on the Trans-Siberian Express from Moscow to Beijing.

I had always travelled and always on my own, but the assault had made me more cautious in many areas. My certainties about myself as independent, invincible – nay, immortal – had gone. The world had become a much more unpredictable, scarier place, and to go round the world alone felt daunting as it never would have before.

Two things convinced me to do it. One was a story I had been told by a traveller at the kibbutz in Israel. He had met a young deaf and mute girl in India who had hitched there from London. On the way she had been raped and badly beaten. He asked her how she had managed to continue and the girl had written down on a napkin:

'Do you think I'm going to let that bastard spoil my trip?'

The man who told me the story said he carried that napkin with him wherever he travelled now.

And yes, why should you let any *bastard* spoil your trip? As well as facing demons, recovering from post-traumatic stress meant claiming back as far as possible that which had wrongfully been taken from me. I did not want to be a victim and I did not want my life to be circumscribed by what had happened. In my autistic world, for all its difficulties, I had been granted certain freedoms and one was the choice to go where I wanted when I wanted without having to consult others. And I wanted to go on the Trans-Siberian very badly.

The other reason that convinced me was horses. I now had something specific in mind: the Trans-Siberian Express passes through Mongolia, the mecca of the horse world. The thought of horses on the Mongolian plains, home to Genghis Khan, the wide open spaces of the steppes, awoke something in me that I could not put in to words. Some years previously I had seen a picture in a magazine of a young Mongolian woman riding the plains in the 1920s. The picture was in black and white but still showed the contrast common in this region of the apple-red cheeks and the nut-brown skin of her face. In the picture her black hair is streaming behind her and she sits her galloping horse with ease, a wide smile suffusing her face. Now I thought I understood why she was smiling – it is the smile we all inwardly wear when we are galloping with ease on a horse, that sense of freedom and exhilaration and happiness that only being on a horse can bring. Another life and the woman could have been me – in many ways I wish it had been. This was one photo I didn't want to airbrush the human face out of.

16

mongolia

On the plain of the yurt camp the strange blue-tinted grass is swaying in the early morning breeze. The steppes spread out endlessly, dotted by their principal inhabitants: sheep, yaks and horses. No human is about yet and I'm listening to that rarest sound of all – silence. It is so silent I can hear the wind, the distant cacophony of grazing beasts making their steppe dawn chorus. In fact, this is not silence at all, just sound filling its natural space.

On the slowly warming plain the horses in the corral down from the yurt camp stand immobile, their hind legs resting, their heads bowed. Only their tails move, idly swishing at the onslaught of the summer flies. But no one stirs, and I stand on the plain, gazing at the receding hills and pasture, and know what space, real space, is for the first time. It stretches away, the emptiness of the steppes which is somehow not empty at all but whole and complete.

Someone emerges from a round white yurt tent.

'G'day.' An Australian traveller stands and looks around.

'Just listen to that,' he calls to me. 'It's so damned quiet.'

The spell is broken.

From the moment of catching the Trans-Siberian Express in Moscow, the train journey here has prepared me for this silence. But first there has been a whirlwind tour of the capital, guided by Elena who speaks perfect English and has read any book I care to mention. As she shows me Red Square, the Kremlin, the Bolshoi, she talks of Pasternak, Mandelstam, Goncharov, Pushkin… I don't tell her that I've not 'done' Pushkin yet, that he is on that ever-extending list of books to read.

'Have you read *War and Peace*?' she asks, her face already expressing doubt. She lights up when I tell her Andrei Bolkonsky was one of my early heroes. 'You're the first person I've ever given a tour to who has,' she says, more in sadness than in anger – for her this is a terrible indictment on the state of the world's education. As a reward for my reading, she tells me, 'I've got something special to show you.'

She takes me to the elegant mansion built in the Muscovite classicism style on Povarskaya Street. 'That was the setting for the Rostovs' house,' she tells me. We gaze at it. Perhaps we are both feeling that frisson of literature brought into real life. Perhaps only I am.

We move on to Red Square, gaze up at the Kremlin and St Basil's Cathedral, and the talk turns to history, the calamitous twentieth century of Russia and the Soviet Union. How to calculate the dead? First World War, Revolution, the Ukrainian Famine, the unthinkable scale of casualties from the Second World War, Stalin's purges, the Holocaust, whose figures were only leaked out belatedly due to the need of Stalin to preserve an image of the Soviet sacrifice as that of one heroic socialist nation. Elena says that, as a Jew, she is still trying to fathom the depths of it. Close to Red Square, a newly married couple and their entourage visit the Tomb of the Unknown Soldier at the

Kremlin Wall in the Alexander Garden. It's a tradition, Elena tells me, a way of thanking those who gave their lives in the 'Great Patriotic War' that people might live in freedom today, marry and be happy.

For your tomorrow we gave our today...

She leaves me at the Moscow underground. As I look up, entranced by the magnificent architecture, she brings me back to earth and below to another kind of underground. 'Built on slave labour,' she says tersely.

Later alone, I wander around the art galleries and Moscow's famous department store, GUM, and sit on the steps of the former Lubianka Prison from which thousands, including Solzhenitsyn, had their fates sealed by a firing squad or on a train heading to Siberia. A rosy-faced, pleasant young policeman comes up and smiles apologetically. 'Izviniche. Neylzya.' *Excuse me. That's not allowed.* He indicates with a wave of his hand that I shouldn't be sitting there. We live, I reflect, in fortunate times.

That evening I too am on a train bound for Siberia. And – joy of all joys – I have a whole sleeping compartment to myself. SARS – the epidemic that never was from China – has driven tourists away in droves. The Trans-Siberian Express is barely half full and I am the lone British traveller amongst a group of German tourists, Russian travellers and the Mongolian traders known as human shuttlecocks who make the endless back-and-forth journeys across the vast expanses of this earth to sell in the markets of Moscow and Beijing.

I embrace the monasticism of my train-compartment cell. Outside, Russia passes before me: the taiga, the endless forests and fields and lakes in a never-ending private viewing. Inside, I read Sholokhov's *And Quiet Flows the Don*, that classic of

Cossack life on the steppes; I sleep, meditate and study my Russian grammar book. I'm a year into my plan to read *War and Peace* in the original Russian, a plan as ambitious and doomed to failure as Napoleon's and Hitler's winter campaigns. Some Russian has been useful, however, for negotiating the Moscow underground, ordering omelette and red wine or borscht and vodka from the Trans-Siberian canteen, pretending to the German tourists that I am not English and thereby obviating the need to talk.

The days slip by as the time zones roll past. On the train we keep Moscow time and a French couple boarding in mid-Siberia ask me why I'm only getting up at four in the afternoon. Facial features slip by too, broad Slavic faces segueing imperceptibly into Asiatic. I get to know the *Provodnik* who sleeps in her lair at the end of my train carriage. Somewhere between a concierge and a prison warder, she guards her compartment fiercely. She is perhaps a yard at the hips; her bosom is a dangerous weapon. When I try to speak Russian to her, she perceptibly melts in gratitude. I never have to beg for hot water again, she gives me sweets, and her set Russian features break into what might be a smile when she sees me.

The days pass and we are at the Mongolian border. As if to welcome our coming, Nature lays on its most spectacular electric blue storm. We watch in awe and wonder from the train windows as lightning illuminates the wild hillsides in flash after flash and thunder drowns out all talk. We stand glued to the train windows – none of us has seen a telly for days.

Over the border, the rain has stopped and the Mongolian police emerge on the tracks, shouting in Russian, 'Have you got any dollars?' I throw down a chocolate bar and one of them catches it deftly. He grins up at me, his face a picture of boyish joy: 'Spasibo' (thank you). This is policing Mongolian-style.

Emerging from the train in Ulan Bator station, I feel a pang, such as a novice might feel on emerging from the novitiate of a convent for the first time. I will miss my cell, the rhythm of the train which now courses through my bloodstream, the silent, private space.

There is a brief period of grace. A guide takes me to a hotel. I am allowed to drop off my luggage, take a shower, and then I must present myself for the tour. I join a group of travellers, mostly Australian, to be shown the Gandan Monastery, Ulan Bator's only department store, Parliament Square. I listen in irritation to talk of where to find the best hotel jobs in London, what to see in Berlin, where the best parties are in Bangkok. I detach from the group on the massive Soviet-style Parliament Square, reading the Cyrillic script on the parliament building, a legacy of communist domination. A group of horsemen ride up on to the square. 'What's that for?' I ask the friendly young Mongolian guide who clearly wishes I'd get a bit more involved with the group, worries that I'm feeling left out. 'It's just people come into town to do some shopping,' she says. I'm enthralled: a capital city where people ride into town to do their shopping and carry out their affairs on horseback. Clearly it is not particularly noteworthy here – you ride into town from your yurt tent and you ride back with your carrier bags full on a horse.

In the afternoon I break rank and wander back to the outer walls of the Gandan Monastery where artists display their watercolour paintings of Mongolia. The artist I speak to has a kind, gentle face, typical of those in this peace-loving Buddhist country. He speaks good English and tells me he lectures on art at the Ulan Bator University. I tell him I want a picture of horses on the steppes. He shows me landscapes of horses and reindeer, of burning deserts and snow-covered mountains. And he talks about art, nature, the interconnectedness of man and landscapes and animals. His pictures are beautiful; he has the simplicity of the truly gifted who have unquestioningly followed an artistic calling. I feel I am in the presence of a true artist. Before I go, he presents me with a free picture, a watercolour of a fat puppy playing in long grass. He smiles and looks directly at me, and for once I don't break the gaze; I look back into his all-seeing, prescient eyes. 'I think you were meant to come to Mongolia,' he says.

Later that evening, as the bus winds through the ugly urban sprawl outside Ulan Bator towards the grasslands of the yurt camp, I'm feeling less sour towards the human din of the other tourists. The horses are getting nearer. This is what I have come for. Along the way, shamanic offerings wrapped in bright blue scarves lie by the roadside. The far-reaching plains take me far away from the noise that we call talk.

Fate seems to have blessed me on this trip. Of all the travellers, I alone have a yurt, the traditional nomadic tent, to myself. I sit inside the round felt tent, supported by wooden slats which can be put up or taken down in less than two hours – a home, like a tortoise's, to carry with you wherever you go. It is heated by its own wood-burning stove, decorated with orange and blue furniture. The wind whistles somewhere outside on the darkening steppes. Heaven.

Later the next morning the sleepy horses in the corral are saddled with the traditional high wooden saddles of Mongolia. Young Mongolians in traditional dress of kaftans, known as deels, are lassoing horses outside the corral using a stick with a lasso rope on the end (the uurga). One squats on his haunches and nods nonchalantly as a young Australian woman asks if she can take his picture.

I'm thinking about Genghis Khan and the Mongol hordes invading the plains, pushing on for domination of the known world. Like so much else, this was only possible due to the horse. Here, out on the steppe lands, man is supposed to have first sat on the horse, leading to the myth of the centaur, the half man, half horse of legend.

The horses are a mixed bunch, varied in height and colour but tending more towards pony size. These descendants of Przewalski's horse, the closest we have to the original wild horse, stand tamely to be saddled and bridled. A young man jumps nimbly onto the back of a more sprightly one; when his back is turned, another young Mongolian with a wicked grin slaps the horse's hind quarters, sending it bucking forward. The rider stays on and laughs at this literal horseplay.

We Western travellers are assigned a horse each. Being small, I am given a dun-coloured pony, smaller than the others. He is quite thin and I worry about his capacity to carry me, but as we set off he streaks ahead of the others and I am called back, back to the group which talks about beer and going back to Australia and rugby. On the semi-arid plain we pass sheep, oxen and yaks. Most of the visitors to the camp are not riders; they are here for a morning stroll. In the afternoon they will go on a farm visit, maybe drink Airag, the national drink made from mare's milk. I want to ride more, outride the inane chatter, the white-noise background hum in a place where there are no white goods.

In the afternoon it is just me and a guide. My guide, Mishell, is about 16 and has a smattering of Russian. He tells me he wants to go to America one day. He is polite and considerate, and his face is open and friendly, a face that trusts and knows the world around it. These preliminaries over, we lapse into a comfortable silence, broken only by the thud of the horses' hooves on the semi-arid grassland, the 'chu-chu' sound of Mishell urging them on. We travel over a dusty plain, through the swaying blue grass. There are no roads to mark the way, no signposts, no other humans. I sense that I could be riding forever into the unknown, like the young woman in the picture. Unexpectedly, over a hillock we come to a lake, our destination.

We stop and rest the horses, dismounting and leaving them to wander into the lake. Despite the warmth and the hours of travelling, they do not drink but stand placidly up to their knees in water, content to stay within this human/horse herd. Mishell skims stones across the water. I try too but don't have the knack. He laughs and shows me how to do it. After several attempts I shout, 'Yes!' as a stone manages three leaps on the surface before sinking. He laughs again and, in the universal language, offers me a high five.

We ride back to the yurt camp in a contented silence, letting the horses find their way.

I ride for several more days until it is time to leave. Before I board the bus, there is a final meeting. The group guide tells me the camp leader wants to see me. He is a tall, older man in traditional clothing. Surrounded by his sons and grandsons, he is very much the patriarch. He takes my hand in his brown, lined ones and smiles, turns to the guide and speaks. She translates:

'He says he's heard you are a good horsewoman. He wants you to come back again next year and ride his own special horse. He says you will always be very welcome in this camp.'

I'm deeply touched and pass on my thanks through the guide. They talk some more, then the leader turns and smiles at me as he speaks and the guide interprets: 'He says he especially wants you to come back for the Naadam, to enjoy the great sports of Mongolia.'

The Naadam is Mongolia's greatest annual festival. It is held in July and celebrates the three manly sports of wrestling, archery and, of course, horsemanship.

I return to Ulan Bator and the Trans-Siberian Express, to travel on past the outskirts of the Gobi desert, with its native wild Bactrian camels, and into China. I have never regretted leaving anywhere so much. The days on the Mongolian steppes have been horse heaven, where I have felt completely at peace with the unasking, beautiful landscape. For the first time since the attack happened, now nearly two years ago, I have not thought of it once.

Sadly, I've not been back for the Naadam yet. I have ridden across other landscapes: the mountains and forests of Transylvania, the Great Plain of Hungary, the lunar, volcanic landscape of Iceland, the beaches of Cadiz, the salty marshes of the Camargue… And each time it came to me more and more strongly – I wanted this every day, wanted the calm, healing presence of horses to be with me every day for the rest of my life. And then I realised something else: I didn't just want horses in my world, I needed them.

The great thing about nearly being killed or dying, if you survive reasonably intact, is that it focusses the mind wonderfully on what really matters, what is important and how you really want to spend the rest of your days. My overriding thought at the time of the assault before I resigned myself to being killed was: *It's too soon – I'm not ready for this – there's still too much to do.*

As I began the journey back to recovery, the realisation that my life hadn't been prematurely snuffed out halfway through brought with it the realisation that the opportunities I hadn't taken to date were still open to me. It was as if I'd been given a second chance to do all those things I'd been denied or, in my closed-off, autistic world, had denied myself. There were still things I could not change because I simply could not deal with them – I knew, for instance, that the majority of social relationships would always be beyond me except at a limited level, but other things were possible, and top of my wish list, enduring for a lifetime, was *a horse*. It was my eight-year-old self's birthday, Christmas and shopping list wish all over again. Only this time there was a chance of getting it.

My relationship with horses was about to enter a whole new dimension, the start of a lifelong journey of openness and discovery, the antithesis of the closed-in, fear-driven world of autism.

Part 3

A Whole New World

17

a horse called bailey

He was a 14.2-hands Connemara cross thoroughbred pony, a slender, elegant boy, more often taken for a mare than a gelding. He had a white, flecked coat (known as flea-bitten grey), was short-backed and powerful with a proud, high-set neck. He had beautiful chocolate-brown eyes, equally beautiful horse manners and – in so far as a human can own another animal – being paid for, passported and possessed, he was mine. And I, apparently, was his.

We stood a little in awe of each other in the stable; *his* stable – *our* stable – no longer for me a theoretical space where horses spend the night, but a real place with real straw for bedding which would need to be mucked out in the morning, a water bucket which would need periodic replenishing, hay nets that would need filling. And I could come here any time I wanted. I was no longer just an envious visitor gazing inwards over a stable door, a visitor to that 'look and touch if you must but never in your wildest dreams think that you will ever possess this' world of horses.

That world had become mine: I had finally inherited the earth. And the conditions of the land deeds terrified me.

This wonderful large beast was now wholly my responsibility: his health, his happiness, his feed, his water, his daily apples, mints and carrots (for already I was hopelessly committed to spoiling him rotten). The responsibilities continued to flood in: shoeing, vets' visits (and bills), rugging and unrugging, grooming, tack cleaning... All this before I had so much as thought about sitting on him. What temerity had I had to invite this level of responsibility into my strange autistic world where most days I couldn't even remember to lock my car door?

This was responsibility indeed, a step into the neurotypical world. Suddenly it came back to me: all that mean, tight-fisted, unfeeling, unthinking, uncaring, parental NO to my pester power for a horse. I now saw the reality behind it.

Unconcerned by any of this, Bailey munched his hay, drawing out long strands from the hay net with powerful teeth, the sound of his macerating jaws filling the stone walls of the stable. I watched him eating, mindful of his space, mindful of this newness to him (it was the day of his arrival), mindful that I had no right to immediate acceptance in his space.

I watched him and worried that I had taken on too much, worried he would not get enough food, worried he would get too much, be too hot or too cold, worried he would die of colic in the night...

Bailey continued eating.

Despite my fears, I had been preparing for this moment for quite a while. Once I had allowed in the possibility that I might get a horse, there was a lot to find out. Now that I was no longer living in the Tooth Fairy world of childhood where ponies could turn up in your bedroom at night and there'd be no vets' bills or mucking out to face in the morning, there were certain things I needed to learn and I wasn't going to get it all from books.

I duly enrolled in some horse-care courses at the local agricultural college. Equine courses were a new growth area. I doubt that any had existed when I was growing up and certainly not ones open to anybody – then you were just born into horses or not. Now, even people like me could study horses at evening classes along with flower arranging, conversational French and wine tasting.

I drove to my first class thinking that I was probably doing this 20 years too late – in terms of horses, I always felt I had missed out, missed any chance of ever getting my foot in the stable door. But again my love of and fascination with all things equine overrode my fears. If I was going to make a fool of myself, at least it would be in a good cause as far as I was concerned. I signed in at college, expecting, if I'm honest about it, to be sitting in a room full of over-privileged, blonde teenage girls in pink jodhpurs with the shared resources of being heiresses to half the county and one brain cell between them. The tutor would probably be called something like Clarissa Wyndham-Smyth, the local squire's daughter in tweeds and pearls, with a posh voice like a foghorn.

I couldn't have been more wrong. There were 12 women there and one man – just ordinary people, some older, some younger than me, all there because of a love of horses. The tutor, Eileen, was a lovely down-to-earth Yorkshire lady with many years' experience of horses, which she was happy to share with those of us who didn't know a fetlock from a forelock or the difference between hay and haylage.

Unknown to me, a quiet revolution had been going on in the demographics of the British equestrian world. Those of us who had spent our childhoods dreaming of that white horse turning up in the bedroom, who had devoted every spare minute and spent precious pocket money on anything and everything to do with horses – everything except the horse, that is, because it was always beyond our reach – had grown up. Boyfriends had come along, university, careers, family for some, and now we had reached a stage of more affluence and more time, and that original love of horses had come back – only now we could afford to have the horse. Horses were no longer in the hands of the privileged few: an explosion in the equine leisure industry, in livery yards – and probably in questioned assumptions too – meant that women in their thirties and forties were returning to horses in – well, herds. The average age of horse riding was no longer between 10 and 15. It was 30 upwards. It was for anyone. It was for me.

I hadn't been in a classroom for a while. Although it was some time on from the assault, the effects of post-traumatic stress made it difficult to go into new situations then; I felt easily stressed, on edge and always had to make sure I knew where the quickest exit was for a getaway. Often now, when away from home, I had an overwhelming urge to be back there and these days I spent much less time outside than inside. I was also not good at learning in groups, struggling to deal with both the demands of learning and being around others at the same time. But in that class I felt fine and, once I'd worked out an escape route in my head, I began to enjoy exploring what was, after all, one of my favourite subjects.

I learned a lot about horse care over the next few months: how to muck out, fill and tie up a hay net, measure out horse feed, bring a horse in from the field, check a horse's temperature, put on a rug... As always, practical, hands-on things didn't come as second nature to me. I could learn things very easily in the abstract or alone and in my own time if I was interested, but when it came to undertaking shared tasks or practical things, I probably fell in a special needs category. I would learn eventually, but it took me more time and the end results were variable. I got used to being asked the following:

'Are you sure you've got that rug on right? It looks like the tail end is where the neck should be.'

'Would you sleep in such a lumpy bed at home?' (I didn't dare answer that one.)

'How long do you think that hay net is going to stay up for?'

'You're supposed to pick out the back hooves as well as the front.'

I didn't mind. I knew I'd get it in the end, and by the time Bailey came I was well versed in the basics of horse care.

Bailey was far too good for me and far more talented than I could ever hope to do justice to then. We met at a horse-training weekend in north Wales where I was learning the rudiments of jumping. Bailey was an affiliated showjumper, had hunted and done one-day events, and he was being sold at the equestrian centre where the course was being held. He was described as a ten-year-old schoolmaster – in other words, a horse suitable for those with less experience to gain more experience. Each morning, before the lessons began, I would go down to see him with an apple I had filched from the kitchen, quartered and cored (as if a horse cares), which I would feed to him in his stable. Bailey would hesitate before taking the apple, as if to say, 'Oh, really, for me? You shouldn't have bothered,' before taking it delicately off my palm and chomping on it until the juice drooled from his lips and a look in his lovely soft eyes said, 'This is heaven.'

I rode him for most of the week and by Friday it was a no-brainer – I loved him and he was coming to live with me. Back home, I arranged for him to go on full livery at a local livery stable, on the premise that if someone with experience looked after him initially, I would gradually learn myself. He travelled on a January day from North Wales and was settled in his new stable on a beautiful yard. The stable was old-fashioned grey stone and built around a small courtyard with a rill running through it. It was on a private estate with extensive woodland and wildlife, including deer. I couldn't believe this was happening to me.

Over those first few months with Bailey, I was to learn the arcane arts of cooperation and partnership and trust as I never had before with humans or, in fact, dogs. Dogs, being generally smaller and more subservient to humans, will acquiesce to the demands of a human alpha male or female (or at least a perceived one) without too much trouble if the conditions are right. It is different with horses, not just because they are biologically programmed very differently to dogs – being prey animals rather than predators – but because horses have an awful lot more weight behind them; should they choose not to cooperate, the potential to squash, maim and kill is considerably higher. It is better therefore to get a horse on your side, which means cooperation and partnership.

These are strange concepts in an autistic world.

With Bailey, I had the freedom to be around a horse completely on my own terms for the first time in my life, and I spent hours just being with him, observing his behaviour, learning his likes and dislikes, starting to understand the interspecies communication between horses and humans. In many ways I had an easy introduction to the world of cooperation and partnership with Bailey: he was a perfect gentleman. He would walk beside me with no need for a head collar and rope; he stepped aside when I wanted to get past him at just a touch from a finger, moved back in his stable when I opened the door to come in and, despite being able to mug me ten times over for a Trebor mint, would respectfully lower his head and wait expectantly whilst I fumbled to bring it out of my pocket. Bailey combined this sensitivity with a gentleness that amazed me. I would have felt safe sleeping in the same stable with him (and if he'd been a man, he would have let me have the best share of the duvet too). He was very subtle in his movements and would tenderly lick me, anywhere and everywhere, for hours. He was an expert at stealing carrots out of my jacket pockets without me noticing, and when I turned to find him secretly munching, his look would be far away, a real 'Who, me?' look. He was nearly subtle enough to steal them out of my jeans' back pocket too, delicately placing his teeth around them so that he didn't touch my bum and slowly, stealthily withdrawing the carrot. I caught him out every time but it always made me laugh – I couldn't get cross with him.

I never had to try to catch him from the field. He would come cantering up to me, whinnying his high-pitched call, and I suspect if he could have put his own head collar on to go with me, he would have. We developed a game in which I would arrive in the drive up to his field in the car; Bailey somehow knew the sound of my car and would be there, standing at the top end of the field, overlooking the dry stone wall, waiting for me. Then we'd have a race with me giving the car full rev down the bumpy track and Bailey galloping for all he was worth towards the gate. I invariably won but I did have several units of horsepower on my side whereas Bailey had only one, so I always gave him a pat and a treat at the gate. It probably didn't do the car suspension any good, but I wasn't that interested in cars anyway. Bailey wasn't the bravest of horses, and if the other horses in the field came to drive him away, I would stand between Bailey and the others and drive them off, whereas if they tried to push him away from me, he would suddenly grow a spine, put his ears back, lower his head and send them packing with a look that said, 'Get away from my mum. She's all mine.'

At that time I was still recovering from post-traumatic stress; the world could sometimes be a scary and uncertain place, added to which I always had to live with the abnormally high levels of anxiety that characterise autism (though Prozac seemed to be particularly beneficial in this regard). Being prey animals, horses are also subject to a level of anxiety to a greater or lesser degree most of the time. As intuitive animals, they can pick up on this in humans – perhaps Bailey found in me someone who was less threatening because I lived in a state in which I felt there was always a potential threat out there; perhaps I felt safe and comfortable with Bailey because he was programmed to share this same anxiety, and thus we complemented each other. One thing was certain: we loved being together, and as our partnership was forged and developed over time, I found myself forming a deep-seated attachment which was in total contrast to my frequent need to cut out and block off human contact in the interests of self-preservation. After a day at the office I went through the same decontamination process that I had always gone through, a closing off from the external world, but this time I was doing it by entering the horse's world and therefore I was not doing it alone. It used to amuse me when people came to see their horses after work and spent most of the time there discussing with the others what work had been like that day or what they were going to do when they went home. To me, that time spent alone in the stable with Bailey in the here and now was precious beyond words.

I began to regard the part of the day that I spent with him as the most important time there was. Horses seem to exist in a time zone of their own, the slow steady roll of natural time where there is no sense of urgency, and the clock-bound, rigid schedules of human time could disappear altogether when I was brushing Bailey or meandering round the school on him or just sitting with him in the field or in his stable. The everyday world, with all its nagging worries and fears and stresses and frustrations, seemed to melt into a seductive, all-absorbing alternative universe, and the consequence was that I went from being a rigidly on-time, anxious, finger-tapping, impatient person to being the one who was late most of the time.

The human tendency to be in the past or the future, or anywhere but the here and now, which is the only place we can actually truly be, is not something the horse recognises. Yes, they bring their baggage from the past, the long-term memory of the person who beat them, the angry farrier who kicked them, the person who took their food away when it wasn't finished – they need that memory to learn and survive – but they don't live in that past, nor do they project on to a possible future, the mapped and planned-out days and weeks and years, with all the anxieties about what may or may not happen (and probably never will). This was to be crucial in terms of processing the post-traumatic stress which had left me caught on a past event, seemingly destined to be endlessly stuck in the moment when I felt I was facing my own destruction, destined to always be an outsider looking in on myself. Whenever I was with Bailey, I came out of that place into the present, and the more time I spent with him, the more I could be in the present and fully inside myself.

To be around horses is to be in the current moment, not let off the world but linked to what is happening in front of us, the annual unfolding of the seasons, the diurnal cycle, the rich grass of summer and the barren mud of winter. Everything has its time and place. The assault had led to me dissociating from myself, but prior to this I had always lived in my own detached, autistic world which remained unconnected to the world around me. With Bailey, the external environment, the season, the earth, the state of the grass, the clouds in the sky all took on a new significance. Prolonged heat meant dry grass, reduced water supplies, flies, sunburn around his eyes and muzzle, and sweet itch on his mane and tail. Snow and frost meant no grass in the field, frozen water supplies, cold at night. Rain (the most likely of all in the north of England) could lead to muddy fields, mud fever on his legs, filthy rugs when he rolled, rain scald. The natural world and its cycles suddenly mattered much more to me because they also mattered to Bailey.

Perhaps my proudest, if not my most special, moment with Bailey came when he met Max, a small Arab gelding.

Years before, when I was at school, we were set the uninspiring task of writing an animal story. Inevitably, I chose to write about horses. The result was a fairly schmaltzy story of waiting for a herd of wild horses on the moor and finally being singled out for attention by the herd stallion (Freudians can make of that what they will). In fact, I probably still didn't know what a stallion was, but I did know that if an animal chose to be with you above the herd, it was a very great honour. Bailey wasn't exactly a wild stallion (although he might have been in his dreams) but he was a herd animal. When Max was put into his field, the two formed an instant bond. Bailey could be quite aloof with other horses, perhaps because he was smaller than them and expected to be pushed around, but with Max it was love at first sight. The two were inseparable, detaching themselves from the main herd and spending hours together in mutual grooming. They had formed their own sub-herd.

Some weeks after his love affair with Max had begun, I turned Bailey out into the field after riding him. Bailey always stayed with me when I first turned him out and this could go on for ages, neither of us wanting to leave. This time he detached from me and went straight to Max. I didn't mind; I watched, feeling pleased that he had an equine friend now as well as me. After an initial sniff at Max, he turned his long graceful neck and looked at me and then gave the high-pitched whinny he always used to call me. He walked over towards me, Max following, and pushed his head against my sleeve and began to lick as if for all the world he was saying, 'We want you in our herd as well – you can be part of us.' It was a long time before we parted at the gate.

But it wasn't all just an easy ride, so to speak. If Bailey was bringing me down to earth in one sense, he was also doing so in other ways. And it hurt. Although we seemed ideally suited on the ground, he was probably not, at that point, the right horse for me to be riding. I was very much a novice and, like most novices, didn't know how much I didn't know. Bailey, on the other hand, was a seasoned showjumper, a quirky, nervous horse under saddle, who could be very calm one minute and very spooky the next. He was probably not helped by having a novice rider on his back, even though, as often happens in the horse-selling world, he had been sold to me as a schoolmaster.

He could change from being a very calm and relaxed ride one minute to having eyes on stalks the next. This was especially so if we were riding out alone without another horse and rider (which, being me, I always preferred to do). I didn't then have the skills for dealing with this, nor could I resolve his potentially dangerous habit of exploding in enormous bucks which seemed to come from nowhere. He could also spin unexpectedly and for no apparent reason, his Connemara and thoroughbred heritage making him very sharp, and staying in the saddle during these episodes was not easy. As a novice rider, it did not do my confidence much good when twice I ended up in hospital. I always limped out determined to carry on riding, but it was taking the pleasure out of it. Being alone with a spooky, unpredictable horse when you don't have the skills to deal with it is frightening. The reality was that, no matter how much I loved him on the ground, he scared me when I was riding him.

I persisted believing it was me (perhaps some of it was, although I was also to witness Bailey unseat much more experienced riders with his out-of-nowhere bucks). I went through the usual checks with horse dentists and chiropractors and saddle fitters, and I religiously went to ride him every day, although sometimes my teeth were chattering at the thought of it and I was thinking to myself that I really should have a will in place (all proceeds would go to a horse sanctuary in the event of my demise). I didn't want to lose Bailey, but he would have been too expensive a pet just to keep as a field ornament and I couldn't bring myself to sell him on. I began to look for solutions.

The result was that I began to focus much more on my riding and how I was affecting him. I had more lessons on him with a lovely lady called Pat who said from the start, 'I don't believe in all this "there are good riders and bad riders". There are just people with more experience than others.' I might have strained Pat's theory a bit, but anyway it was reassuring to hear that. You can't suddenly enter the horse-riding world as an adult and hope to be as good as people who've been doing it from the age of four. Pat's words gave me permission to be where I was in the learning phase, and also taught me that progress only comes from practice and experience: it was OK to be a novice, OK to be learning things for the first time. It was a total contrast to my usual way of learning in which I would either grasp things very quickly or not bother to learn them at all. It taught me patience and it taught me humility.

Riding was not something that came naturally to me: so much time spent in a cerebral world militated against it. With Bailey, maybe I was trying too hard for that 'perfect position', as if one position exists in a process that is dynamic and fluid. Maybe I was still not fully inside myself or was instinctively tensing up in anticipation of one of Bailey's sudden antics. Anyway, I decided that if I wanted Bailey to relax, I was first of all going to have to try to relax a bit more myself. Being highly intense and fixated when I'm concentrating on doing something, this wasn't easy. I bought a hypnosis tape which focussed on relaxed riding and played it over and over before I went to sleep – usually I fell asleep while listening to the tape and only came round at the end during the countdown to wake up, but, anyway, during my absence something seemed to have happened because I began to relax on Bailey a lot more. The tape encouraged deep breathing, much as the EMDR psychologist had done. This time, however, I had more of an incentive to try it – the fear of a hard landing if I didn't. Looking back, I think it did help a lot. Tension around animals as sensitive as horses rarely achieves much and I had to learn to let everything go and relax, especially at the point where I thought Bailey was about to spring something on me (this is not always easy when that 'something' can land you in the wake of a ten-ton truck).

I learned to breathe deeply, speak calmly and scratch his withers to reassure him. Bailey seemed to respond well to the sound of my voice and seemed to like listening to stories as we rode out. We had a repertoire I would relay to him as we rode along – episodes from *Black Beauty*, *Sea Biscuit* (a particular favourite) and *National Velvet*. Probably it just worked because Bailey was reassured by the sound of my voice and I was distracted from worrying by trying to remember the plot line of what happened after Ginger was sold. Anyway, I was eventually confident enough to ride him out alone and we started to enjoy blasts together along bridleways and across Pennine moorland which always left me laughing for joy. I was entering the world of the Mongolian horsewoman.

Bailey taught me about different coping mechanisms and how to think about and be responsive to another sentient being. In the process I had also learned that I was no longer a sole operator. When riding, there are, *ipso facto*, two of you in the equation. It was no longer possible to retreat into the inner isolation of autism; partnership means doing things together, being responsible for how your actions affect another. For better or for worse, for the time I was riding I was sharing this world with another. Effectively, I was using my body language to calm him and, to my surprise, it worked – when I was on him, I was not just an isolated individual who had no connection with anyone else.

Some years later I traced Bailey's original owner via information that came with his passport. A very nice lady answered the phone and was delighted to hear news about Bailey, whom she had bought as a youngster and who had been ridden by her daughter to a high level. One of the first things she said to me was: 'I would have loved to have kept him when my daughter grew out of him, but I could never stick on him. He used to put in massive bucks for no reason.'

So it hadn't just been me. He had come from a very experienced showjumping home and apparently it was something he had always done as a youngster on the hunting field and in the jumping arena, the sort of thing only a talented and fearless teenager could stay with and probably enjoy.

We both agreed that there was something quirky about Bailey, as with most talented horses. He was an enigma and also still the most wonderful horse in the world. I was about to find out just how wonderful.

18

relapse

A few years later I had moved on to some extent from the assault. I could more or less go out of my own front door without having to think about it too much, the scars on my body were fading, and I no longer felt that I was living outside of myself.

In a large measure this was thanks to Bailey. Bailey was the reason I got up in the morning, the reason I went outside every day, whatever the weather; he was that welcome presence always waiting for me at the end of the day, every day, and it was a presence I loved to be in more than anything else. At home and in my immediate environment the dogs continued to enhance my life too, with their unwavering quiet acceptance, their warm welcoming presence in my isolated world.

In other ways, though, things had changed as a result of the assault. Seeing a stranger of a certain height with a shaven head could still see me diving for cover. Spending time away from home could be difficult, and I had to face the fact that my implicit faith in a basically safe universe had gone. I had learned that our world can be knocked from under us at any time, that we are not immortal or special or protected against our own death, and it made me see the world differently. No amount of shoring up against our ruin, as Eliot puts it, can protect us in the long run.

I continued to have nightmares sometimes and one in particular haunted me: a mother telling me I had killed her son. I told no one about it; it seemed too shameful and also on some level I knew it was illogical. But it festered inside me.

I was still on Prozac which kept my moods on a fairly even keel and didn't seem to have any particularly negative side effects. It also helped me cope at work by lowering my ever-present anxiety levels and helped me to tolerate the endless grating effect that being around others for long periods invariably caused. I was now doing a more office-based job and ran groups with offenders on a weekly basis. Working with offenders wasn't problematic on the whole, but I was working full-time which was draining and depleting, and work always took far more out of me than it ever put back in. From what I can gather, most people go to work and gain some benefits from it above and beyond a pay cheque at the end of the month, whether it is socialising or having a structure to the day or feeling oneself to be useful in some capacity. For me, having to be around people for a set number of hours, whether I wanted to be or not, was always very difficult. It wasn't that I didn't work with some extremely nice and often exceptional people; I just wanted to be in my inner autistic world all the time and I knew I couldn't be. I was happy up to the moment I stood outside the office door and then my heart sank, knowing that for the next eight hours I would be feeling like a prisoner marking off time. I constantly daydreamed of being back with Bailey and the dogs or, if it was cold and rainy in winter, of being at home reading about whatever my latest obsession was and cursing work for so rudely interrupting me in its pursuit. Once outside work, alone again after my eight-hour sentence, I was immediately happy.

Even though Prozac was helping me on some levels, I was impatient with it. It had been prescribed to cope with post-traumatic stress and I was still on it more than three years later. My reasoning went that Prozac was holding me back, leaving me feeling numb in some ways, no longer able to really experience stronger feelings or to feel that I was fully alive. Out of impatience, I made the decision to come off the tablets and, as always, did it off my own bat without consulting anyone. Everything seemed fine for about six weeks – presumably because it was still in my system – but then things started to go badly wrong. True, I was feeling more but they weren't the kind of feelings I wanted to have. At first I felt edgy, ready to snap about things, trivial or otherwise. I started to feel unreasonably angry and then upset about nothing in particular.

To make matters worse, I was transferred to a new office at work and was liking it even less. I don't like offices generally, finding them unnatural and often boring places, my preference always being for fields and open spaces or the privacy of my car or my own front room. Getting up in the morning became a serious struggle which I would put off till the last minute, and walking into the new office, which was bigger and where people stuck to certain cliques, revolted me. I detested the whispering exclusiveness of the younger element in the office but was too new to feel part of the 'adult' section. One or two people were really kind, but most probably just didn't know what to make of me. I sat at my desk alone and wanted to be anywhere but there. On one occasion, discussing some routine issues in my manager's office, I burst into tears. It was out of character and I think she was as surprised as I was embarrassed. I told her I hated being there and she promised to try to get me moved. In the meantime, I continued to stare at my computer, just wanting to be somewhere else.

One day I woke up and, as always in that period, wished I hadn't. I stared at the wall and the minutes ticked by; I wasn't going anywhere. It wasn't really any different from staring at the computer, but at least I didn't have to get out of bed to do it. That morning, not even Bailey was going to make me do that. Staring at the wall seemed the only thing worth doing, but as I stared at it, it occurred to me that there was something else I'd like to do: not live. I was feeling, as I would from time to time, worn down by my aloneness, by the never-shared burden of having to do everything for myself. I was tired of it all, weary to death of having to function like a normal person in a world whose norms I did not share, whose rationale I barely comprehended. Perhaps also I was experiencing a delayed response to post-traumatic stress, the additional burden of living in an uncertain universe, having to negotiate a world which was now not just socially challenging but also potentially dangerous and untrustworthy. With a massive effort, I picked up the phone and told my boss I would rather drive off the edge of a cliff than ever work in that office again. Then I continued to stare at the wall.

I spent the next six weeks debating my continued existence. I was filled with inertia, not eating again, and the days just mumbled past in a grey unremitting haze. Bailey was on full livery at the stable yard so I knew he would be fed, watered, turned out into the field and mucked out daily. I worked out a plan for his and the dogs' future in case I ceased to be around and meanwhile I stayed inside and spent most of my time curled up in bed or on the sofa, my face buried in Dessie's soft, still puppy-like fur. Were it not for the dogs, I would have been completely alone during this time.

It was days later when I finally summoned up the energy one evening to go to see Bailey in his stable. He let out a long delighted whicker when he saw me and began pacing at the stable floor, eager to get to me. I didn't want to ride and doubt I could have found the will to do it anyway: I felt shaky and weak from lack of food and from having done so little for so long. I opened his stable and curled up in a corner on the straw, taking in that wonderful horse smell again. On a small level, just that made me feel a bit better; it was like snuggling your face into a comforting blanket. Looking up at Bailey's long arching neck, his soft brown eyes, I didn't say anything, but I didn't need to: horses communicate all the time and they never say a word.

As I sat on the floor, he lowered his head and placed his soft velvet muzzle on my knees and began endlessly licking my hands. Bailey loved to lick – he was more like a dog in that respect. He would lick my jacket, my hair, my face if I'd let him; it was hard to say who groomed whom most. I stroked him behind his softly twitching ears. It was a favourite spot for him – he would always lean into a scratch behind his ears or under the chin.

I don't know how long I sat, but Bailey never stopped licking me or moved away to eat his hay. Darkness came down but we stayed together, his soft muzzle breathing warmly, gently over me. When I rose to go, it was so dark I couldn't see the bolt on the stable door and I was stiff from remaining immobile for so long. But I felt different. I had entered the 'horse zone' – a place of peace and connection set apart from human time and the nagging stresses of the world outside. Just by sitting with Bailey, a minor transformation had taken place. By the time I got back home the feeling had gone but it had been a moment of reprieve.

The next time I saw Bailey he was out in his field. He had heard my car and had already detached himself from the herd and was whinnying at the fence when I pulled up. I didn't want to play a racing game with him tonight. I climbed over the fence into the field and he lowered his head and nuzzled me gently, his big eyes soft and warm, but tonight they had a questioning look and his ears flicked slightly as he sniffed me.

I moved my arm slowly, breaking out of my body's frozen, numb state, and reached my hand along his shoulders and up to the withers. He nickered softly and turned his head to lick my face, then he nudged me gently as if he was inviting me to do something. He moved closer and slowly dropped a foreleg so that his withers were lowered. He was inviting me to get on him – someone somewhere must have taught him that trick in the past, but he had never shown it to me before. The fence was still behind me; I climbed up two rails of it in a backward movement and, reaching across his withers, swung myself on to his back. His ears flickered back to me as if unsure about the unfamiliar feel of a human unmediated by a saddle. It felt strange to me too – I had never sat on him bareback before, and now I felt myself wholly in contact with him, feeling the warmth and breathing of his sides, the powerful bone of the spine and the softest, most gentle living energy imaginable.

He stood stock-still and just let me sit there. I leaned forwards on his neck and buried my face in his mane, grasping it between my hands. I looked down at the horse hooves beneath me and the green grass beneath the hooves, and as I looked down, I realised I was crying. I fought back the tears, clenching my teeth and angrily brushing them away, as I would brush flies off Bailey. But they kept coming from a place so deep inside me I didn't know it existed, one that might have been there a long time ago but had been so overgrown by the need to move on and survive that I had forgotten it.

And suddenly I was sobbing from the depth of my being, for all my aloneness in the world and the struggle it had brought, for all the absences that I could never fill in my autistic universe – the homes to go to, the warmth and security and nurturance that they implied and that would never be mine. And I carried on sobbing for all the silences that had smothered my needs, for all the wasted years spent living in a world where I could not and never would belong. It came pouring out of me in sobs that felt as if they would never end, the pent-up hurts of a lifetime shaking and ricocheting through me as I sat on Bailey. He remained still and then bent his neck round. Clutching his mane blindly, I slipped off his back on to the ground and crouched in front of his hooves. He looked down at me, lowered his softly curving neck and stood over me, the way a mare will sometimes arch over her foal. I took his face in my hands, cupping both his cheekbones, and laid my head against his long face.

I don't know how long we stayed there. In my self-enclosed world, crying usually made no sense. We cry because we want help or at least because there is the memory or possibility of help somewhere out there. We cry because we take pity on ourselves, but in my universe I could only think in terms of survival, which leaves little room for self-pity. We cry because there is someone there to care about it.

Bailey had been there, and in that unmediated space between him and me I had not been alone. Crying had not just been a pointless, endlessly echoing howl into an uncaring universe.

Bailey silently reaching his head down to me, seeming to share in or care about my grief, was another of those spontaneous acts that have redeemed my world in a way in which anything more would have been overwhelming and terrifying.

He was still standing by the fence, looking for me, when I drove away.

On my doctor's advice I went back on Prozac. Maybe it wasn't ideal to feel a bit numbed off and distanced from myself, but I felt that in the interlude above I had been able to connect with and process some of the complicated and crippling feelings that I'd been holding at bay. To live with these all the time was not good. I had to accept again that nothing was going to change the issues that came with living in an autistic world and also that the effects of post-traumatic stress can be very long: I was always going to be cut off and alone to some degree and the world would never be a wholly safe place to be in. For better or for worse, that was the reality I had to live with and, thanks to horses, it was now a considerably better place than it had been before.

I returned to work reluctantly. A few weeks after, I caught up with some good friends who I had worked with. Rosy and Karen had both worked as psychiatric nurses before going into the Probation Service. My 'oddness' had never fazed them. Although our paths had diverged and there had been long absences when we didn't see each other, we had always stayed in touch and they were two of the very few people I felt comfortable being with and talking to. They hadn't known about the episode of depression, and when I briefly mentioned it over a few drinks, Rosy said to me: 'I hope you'll come and talk to us if it ever happens again.'

'You wouldn't have wanted me around,' I said. 'I just stared at the wall most of the time.'

'It doesn't matter. Come and stare at the wall with us – you don't have to say anything.'

Her words stayed with me. I hadn't approached anyone other than professionals such as my GP, because in my world view I had had no sense of there being anyone there unless they were there with me in the here and now, and even if they were, there was no guarantee they would want to know anything about what was going on. I lived in a world of isolation, but it wasn't always because there weren't friends there or because people didn't care about me.

This episode of depression, plus my time spent with Bailey, led me to look at things again. I wasn't happy working full-time with little time for anything else, even though I was in a relatively well-paid job with good conditions – it was too difficult to balance this with my overriding need for private space. More and more I felt that my real source of fulfilment and happiness came from horses. If there was one thing I could guarantee, it was that the daily hour or however much time I spent with Bailey would always be the best time of the day. I had got him because I wanted to enjoy that feeling more than once a week in an hour's riding lesson. Now I wanted more time every day to enjoy that feeling.

19

the herd

'Hear that, Bailey?'

The muffled, rhythmic knocking of a woodpecker echoed somewhere up in the trees. At the sound of my voice, Bailey cocked a single grey ear back to where I was sitting on his back. He had heard the woodpecker, heard so much more than I ever would, but in trying to share his world I came closer to it. We walked on across the woodland estate, the four-time beat of the horse's hooves making their steady, soothing clip-clop. I fell naturally into the rhythm, counting the beats in my head, my hips swaying with each stride so that we were walking as one, half horse, half human.

I had been with Bailey for several years now and over that time I had learned to see and experience the world differently – see it and hear it as far as I could through his eyes and ears, take on the horse's prey perceptions. I learned about how he was witnessing and experiencing the world as an equine, imagining myself in his place, doing that thing that autistic people find so difficult – putting yourself in someone else's shoes. Except with horses it made much more sense.

By the time I got Bailey I had spent so long alone with dogs that it was second if not first nature to tune in to them, to register their feelings, to observe the slightest twitch of the ear or the nose, interpret the different registers of a bark or yowl. I was more adept at this than I was at picking up human cues, and when horses began to enter my world, a whole new dimension of non-verbal communication, with a subtlety unimaginable to humans, had begun to open up to me. Bailey's willingness to communicate across his world to mine, to share the prey-animal world with a potential predator bespeaks a generosity that no human should ever have the right to expect.

When riding Bailey, I had started to listen in a different way. So often I had felt or been made to feel guilty about my silence, my lack of need for social communication, but being with Bailey, riding through natural landscapes where there is no inane chatter, I felt my silent world vindicated. Silence allows us to tune in to other energies which may equally be telling us something; it allows us to feel, to read body language (which paradoxically accounts for the vast majority of communication anyway), and our own silence allows us to listen. Although largely silent, horses listen and feel endlessly: they can hear the distant rustle of grass in the wind, feel the approach of another horse from far off through their hooves, detect the wing movement of a fly landing on their back. They are endlessly aware of external stimuli, as anyone who has ever observed the constant twitching and flickering of a horse's ears can testify. Riding Bailey, I came to understand the need to remain aware of external noise – at an instinctual level his survival depended on it. I learned therefore that not all noise was bad and I learned the importance of acknowledging external stimuli, the purpose it served in the self-preservation mechanisms of a prey animal whose world I was sharing.

I was starting to see things differently too. Horses look at the world with near 360-degree vision through large eyes situated at the sides of their heads, taking a sweeping view of the environment, ever watchful for potential predators on the horizon. When I was riding Bailey, I had had to consciously start taking in a lot more of the world around me to understand his world view, allowing my eyes to soften and take in peripheral vision. My more instinctive response to block the world out and focus internally as a way of keeping anxiety at bay was being challenged. With Bailey, I shared that anxiety and the watchfulness it entailed, and by seeing the world through other eyes, *his eyes*, I was able to reappraise it – was that person on the horizon really any more threat to me than the fluttering piece of newspaper that Bailey spooked at? This reappraisal played a significant part in teaching me to become more aware of my surroundings, able to see and be part of something other than the autistic world I lived in, able to be more rational and less feral in assessing a perceived human threat.

We walked out of the woodland, climbing higher and higher up on to gorse-covered moorland, scaring away nesting birds, crushing the ever-resilient heather which will spring back time and time again to bring its purple spread of flowers each year. We travelled up the rutted moorland tracks, rising above the treeline. Pausing to give Bailey a rest and a chance to graze, I looked down on a flock of grey-white birds circling beneath us, changing direction as one in a silver, shimmering morphic field. Watching them move in time with each other, effortlessly and silently reading each other's cues and turns, is a magical moment, a witnessing of that silent but ever-communicating world around us.

Bailey had brought me here to this eagle's position, a bird's eye view of a bird's eye view, and it was only one of the everyday natural miracles that I was constantly witnessing and experiencing on horseback. Whilst I gazed around me, Bailey munching the coarse moorland grass growing by the dry stone walls, I reflected on how much I owed him for bringing this beautiful natural world to me. True, I had walked the dogs in it before getting him, but with the dogs it was often a case of just letting them off the lead and leaving them to their own devices, whilst I stomped across the moors, my head down, my thoughts elsewhere, thinking of something that was not in the immediate present, oblivious to the amazing spread of nature before me. It was different with horses. You remain together throughout the ride (or at least that is the plan), your position is much higher, your vision is much broader, and with Bailey I had learned to tune in to the landscape as never before. I watched the natural world, listened to it, observed its changes: I looked out for the first thrusts of green grass through mud in spring, welcomed the healing willow herbs and cursed the poisonous ragwort in summer; I noted the windfalls of apples to harvest for Bailey in autumn and the stark beauty of black winter trees against early red sunsets.

Bailey's ears were relaxed, trusting me to keep watch whilst, head down, he ate, to sound the alarm at any approaching predator. On other occasions, he would keep watch for me, communicate in his horse way that there was danger and that we needed to move. We got by on this easy symbiosis, a shared understanding which needed no words. We shared our talents and abilities too. For the time we were riding together I borrowed his strength, his power, the athleticism that made light of the steep Yorkshire hills; he carried me across fords and streams, he put on a fast spurt to get us both home when caught out in the rain or the hail or the snow. In turn, I brought to him my understanding of the human world which he had to negotiate, the knowledge that a low-flying plane was not a prehistoric pterodactyl come to swoop on him; I shared the cleverness of my human hands which could open gates and remove stones from his feet, brought to him resources of feed and water and shelter and hay when we returned. We had melded our worlds into a different but equal partnership.

It had taken time to reach this point, but the journey had been enlightening. With Bailey, I had moved from my closed-off world into his and I had done so willingly. I had spent hours in the field and stable, watching how Bailey and the other horses interacted, learning their subtle communication skills, seeing how a flicker of an ear, the stance of the neck, the expression in the eyes or activity of the tail could all contribute to and regulate the herd behaviour without a word being spoken. It was an extension of what I had done with the human species all my life – observe and imitate and try to process an understanding of it, whilst never being wholly part of it. Now my human watching skills were starting to pay off, standing me in good stead to observe and imitate and share the ways of a different species. I did not bring to horses the anthropomorphic assumption that they would think and see the world as I did or that they would speak my language and that they were stupid if they didn't.

It was on this particular ride, observing the birds in flight and breathing in the pure moorland air, that I began to think about maybe getting another horse. Until now it had just been Bailey and me. With humans, I had always shied away from groups; in fact, dealing with more than one other person at a time was likely to overwhelm me and send me withdrawing as I felt myself being split by the additional demand, spread too thin and fragmented. I invariably felt that in a gathering of more than two I would be the least welcome person there anyway, but as horses did not overwhelm me, I began to reason that perhaps there was room for more than one, that what I gained from Bailey could be doubled, not diminished, by adding another horse. I was fully aware that, as with humans, I would never really be a fully paid-up member of any herd or group, but with horses I was prepared to settle for an honorary membership if they had the grace to let me in.

And they did.

When the chance to buy some stables and rent some land in the Yorkshire Dales came up, I leapt at the chance. I was well versed in the care and ways of horses by now. I knew that horses tended to thrive best if they were kept as nature intended them (unless they had been bred in a specific way) and that horses' needs boil down to a few essentials: food, water, company, exercise and shelter. I wanted somewhere to keep Bailey where he could live as naturally as possible, so when the land and stables came up, I was ready to move.

I also wanted, as always, to be in my own space, to not have to be around other horse owners if I chose not to be. Not that there was anything wrong with them; I just preferred not to have the time I spent with Bailey interrupted by other people talking about other things, making what I regarded as that endless pointless noise that only humans make. I wanted the time I spent around horses to be unmediated by the distractions of a human presence.

Horses are herd animals and to be happy a horse needs company. I needed to get Bailey a friend to share the field with, and that's how Misty came along. Misty was the same age as Bailey, an inch or two shorter at the withers and several inches wider at the chest and barrel. He was a cob/Appaloosa cross and one of the oddest-looking horses I had ever seen. When I first saw his picture as I trawled the internet in search of another horse, what struck me most was his resemblance to the original Przewalski horse of Mongolia. He had a short, spiky Mohican mane (a bit like the Fjord mane in my *Observer Book of Horses and Ponies* all those years ago) and a short, thick-set neck. He was stocky and unrefined, white with dark grey on his legs and face, had brown ears and, true to Appaloosa colouring, had very dark bluish-looking eyes with pink and spots around his eyelids and muzzle. He wasn't handsome or elegant; he had several conformation faults, including a short neck and straight stifles, and his body shape was distinctly barrel-like – in fact, people have been known to laugh when they first see him – but for me it was love at first sight. I couldn't believe how sweet he looked and he turned out to have a nature to match. As Mark Rashid has famously said, a good horse is never a bad colour.

Although he had been ill-treated or neglected in the past, which made him wary of men and gave him a tendency to be whip-shy, Misty was still able to form deep attachments. He was a relaxed, easy-going horse in contrast to Bailey. He had a long, easy walking stride which was as comforting as a rocking horse and invariably brought my anxiety levels down to zero when riding. Misty could always be calmed by the sound of your voice or a scratch on his withers, not that he needed calming much. In the early days, having ridden past tractors, heard low-flying helicopters, walked calmly through a herd of disgruntled-looking cattle and stood stock-still at a railway crossing as an inter-city train hurtled past, I came to the conclusion that, in terms of riding, Misty was probably the horse I should have had first, whereas Bailey was definitely more of what is termed in riding a *second horse*.

Bailey didn't take long to establish his position as top of the horse hierarchy. Having been a low-ranking horse in previous groupings at livery stables, he relished the chance to be the alpha male and with Misty he found no opposition. Misty opted for an easy life, not particularly bothered if he was fed first or second, as long as he was fed. Like Bailey, he loved mints, and if Bailey ever wasn't there, being down the field eating, Misty would play a game with me, nosing at my pockets and pretending to bite by smacking his soft velvet lips together against me until he got a mint. It made me laugh, but it also reminded me of how horses can choose to be so gentle: if Misty had ever actually bitten me, he could easily have taken off my fingers.

The fields extended to about three acres, bordered by dry stone walls, and overlooked a river valley with wonderful views of the Yorkshire Dales beyond. I sat for hours on the field, watching the clouds roll over the glorious landscape, learning to be still, to do nothing, to just be there with the dogs and my two lovely horses in my own private field.

There was more than enough grass for Bailey and Misty, and to prevent them getting too fat I began to wonder about getting another pony. At first I had felt disloyal to Bailey for getting Misty, for allowing another horse into that special relationship. Maybe Bailey was a little jealous too – he wouldn't let Misty come close to me if he was there and I had to work out a complicated system which involved making a fuss of Bailey first, taking him into the stable, spending time with him, feeding him and then leaving him to eat whilst I went to tell Misty how much I loved him too. It worked by and large. Bailey was always going to have first call on me and it was better just to work around this than make him cross and jealous. But anyway, I reasoned, I couldn't be with Bailey all day but Misty could, and I knew Bailey wouldn't be happy on his own all day, so on some level they meant a lot to each other.

Having got over feelings of guilt towards Bailey, it was relatively easy to get another herd member. However, in order not to overload the field with horses and because I had two horses that I could ride, I searched for something considerably smaller.

Alfie was a miniature British Spotted Pony. He was approximately the size of an average Shetland pony, being 36 inches at the withers with a pure white coat and a sprinkling of black spots. He came to me from North Wales as a four-year-old. My first memory is of seeing him alone in a stable, quietly munching at his bedding. In fact, everything about him was quiet – he seemed almost unnaturally still, his movements were very slow and deliberate – but he gently raised his little spotty muzzle to me over the stable door and I was smitten. Instinct was telling me this was a 'good 'un', and when you find a good horse or pony, there's only one thing to do…

Alfie joined the herd.

I introduced him gradually to Misty and Bailey, letting them sniff over the wall and over the stable partition as they slowly got used to each other. At some point, however, you have to bite the bullet. I released Alfie into the field with them and watched, waiting to see how the herd dynamics would arrange themselves. Horses are intensely hierarchical; it's a hangover from the wild where groupings form and defer to the lead mare and stallion. In the wild, the lead horses have a big responsibility to keep the herd safe; in the domestic sphere, it can often just be a pain in the neck with lots of kicking and biting as they jockey for position.

Things seemed to be going well with Alfie. After some initial muzzle-sniffing and squealing (squealing, as always, coming mainly from Bailey), they began to groom. Most horses like to groom each other's withers, often standing head to tail and resembling a two-headed horse whilst they softly gnaw at the parts that the horse can't reach on himself. Alfie was too small to groom the withers of either Bailey or Misty, so he contented himself with gnawing at their shoulders. It made me smile. Alfie was doing his level best to fit in. After a while of this they started to graze and all seemed well. I decided to leave them to it.

When I returned later to give the evening feeds, I could only see Misty and Bailey in the lower field. I wasn't too concerned; this being the Yorkshire Dales, the slope of the field and the dips by the dry stone wall meant that Alfie could easily be concealed in a dip or behind a tree. I called for him and then went looking. I don't know at what point I started to worry – probably at the point at which it became irrevocably evident that there were only two horses in the field and they were Misty and Bailey. My first thought was that Alfie had been stolen – he had the 'aww' factor to the nth degree and it was impossible for people to see him without wanting to keep him. I felt a horrible wave of fear go through me. It occurred to me that perhaps he had run away, jumped the field, and that I would never see him again. It was probably not very likely, given the strong herding instinct amongst equines, but I had only had Alfie a week and he had had little opportunity to fully bond and become part of Bailey and Misty's herd. I feared most of all that, if I never saw him again, I would never know he was all right and safe and warm and fed and looked after (much as I had initially feared for Ollie all those years before). It would haunt me for the rest of my life if that happened.

Once I had thoroughly established he was not in the field, I walked slowly up into the top field, numb and not knowing what to do. Over the wall I saw the farmer who owned the adjacent fields and fear made me break out of my autistic bubble to call out to him, asking him if he had seen a small spotty pony. He said he hadn't but would look out for me. It was small reassurance. I carried on walking to the top of the field and then suddenly I heard a soft nicker. A little spotty pony came walking slowly towards me from out of a dip in the field. I nearly wept with relief.

Clearly Alfie had jumped out of the bottom field. He had a small cut on his foreleg but what bothered me more were the bite marks on his back. He had lumps of hair missing and in some places the skin was broken. I knew it was Bailey who had done this and for the first time ever I felt really angry with him. As well as anger, though, I felt guilty for exposing Alfie in the first place, for not being there to protect him. I made a fuss of him with treats and gave him some feed before putting some soothing lotion on his bite marks. Alfie, in the way of horses, seemed grateful to me, saw me as a friend in what had been an unfriendly environment. He always attached to me far more than to other horses after that. I think he was probably naturally aloof with other horses and they didn't seem to bond with him much either. Like Bailey, he appeared to prefer people, maybe seeing them as his protectors in a world where to be small can make you vulnerable.

I worried for some time that there was something wrong with Alfie. I had never known a horse or pony so quiet. His movements seemed to happen in slow motion; even his eating was a very slow, protracted affair. Eventually, I came to accept this as just how he was, and there have been some definite advantages to it. He remained the sweetest little pony, always happy to just stand still and be cuddled or to raise his head to nuzzle. He was that one-in-a-million pony that everyone looks for and that is so hard to find.

But the reality was he did not fit into the herd. Not Bailey's herd, anyway. Bailey continued to bully him, and although they eventually reached an uneasy compromise, I decided that it might be better to get Alfie a little herd of his own.

Enter Spot.

I had looked at pictures of Spot on the internet for some time. He was a two-year-old miniature British Spotted Pony with unusual chestnut-coloured spots all over him (technically known as red leopard spot). He was born in South Wales and I took the not always recommended step of buying him unseen. He was transported up to Yorkshire and arrived one evening just as it was getting dark.

'He's been a little gem,' the man who transported him said to me. 'Good as gold. No problem at all. A real joy to bring.' It seemed like a good omen. Spot's registered breed name was *Joy Gem Gold Glitter*.

I loved Spot from the start. He wasn't a model pony like Alfie; in fact, in the early days he could be quite pushy and opinionated. But he was a character who endlessly made me laugh, whose butter-wouldn't-melt expression spread all over his cute little dish face belied a strong will and a determination way out of proportion to his miniscule 34 inches.

As a youngster, Spot had two modes of operating which were (1) eat it and (2) if you can't eat it, destroy it. He preferred on the whole to eat, but his capacity for just wrecking everything he came into contact with was impressive. I kept him in the top field with Alfie, leaving Bailey and Misty to get on with it in the bottom field. Although Alfie was fairly indifferent to other horses, I think he liked having something his own size to play with or at least to boss around. As the older, bigger (by two inches) pony, Alfie was automatically elevated to herd boss. It was interesting to watch him teach Spot what was and was not acceptable in horse-herd behaviour, and I learned a lot from just observing it as well. Interloping humans are not always the best teachers of different species, whatever we like to think, however much our egos elevate us to the top of the animal kingdom.

As part of my routine, I would turn the horses out and then muck out the stable. The stables were in the top field and, after feeding, Spot, who was infinitely sociable, would always join me as I mucked out.

'Have you come to help?' I would ask him softly as he poked his tiny muzzle into the stable before walking in. It was like a private joke between us. Spot's version of helping was to wreck everything I had done. As soon as the bedding was mucked out, he would go and poo on it; when the water bucket was filled, he would knock it over. He would go and roll on the newly laid bedding, sending it everywhere, and he had a knack of untying hay nets to bring them down to his own height. This was a process we went through every day – I came to accept it in the end.

As the smallest and youngest in the herd, Spot was always last to get fed; if he attempted to feed before the others, they would rudely push him away. I suspect that this had happened in his previous home too, because Spot had perfected the art of rugby-scrumming into the feed shed whenever the door was opened. Even though I would only open it fractionally to get out the food, he would force his head in with all his might, determined to get at the feed bin – Spot would have tackled the entire All Blacks singlehandedly if it meant first go at the feed bucket. When the others had had their feeds, he would block my way, determined to get the bucket off me before anyone else could steal it off him. It was some time before he came to accept that he would be fed anyway and didn't need to try to force it off me. As a two-year-old, Spot was still learning about boundaries and acceptable behaviour. Once, in a stroppy moment, he turned his back end on me and threatened to kick. I rose to my full height over him (not difficult actually) and shouted at him; he backed off, palpably frightened. He never did it again. I mention this because it is so easy to let small ponies get away with things which then become a normal part of behaviour. What appears cute and funny in youngsters and small ponies is not at all cute or funny when they are bigger and older or left around small children or vulnerable people. I was once given this advice: 'Treat a small pony like a 16-hand stallion and you won't have any problems.' There are behaviours we won't allow in bigger animals because it is too dangerous; not allowing them in smaller ponies prevents a lot of problems too. Ensuring that Alfie and Spot learned manners and respect around people was to be crucial for the future.

Unlike Alfie, Spot was accepted fairly easily by Bailey. At their first meeting I watched apprehensively, waiting to step in if things went wrong. Both Bailey and Misty trotted up to Spot who stood still and raised his muzzle as if for all the world to say, 'I'm Spot. Who are you?' Bailey looked positively taken aback at such confidence in this squirt but sniffed him and squealed. Maybe because Spot was such a youngster, Bailey didn't even feel he was worth bothering with, but I never noticed any problems between them. Misty and Spot lived out together for Spot's first winter (like some Appaloosas, Misty suffered from night blindness which could make him panic if enclosed in a small area in the dark, so he lived out permanently and was quite happy with it), whilst Bailey and Alfie were stabled. Misty very much took Spot under his wing, acting like a benevolent uncle, and the two were inseparable, even though Spot must have tried Misty's enormous patience to breaking point. Just one of Spot's tricks was to wait till Misty raised his head from eating from his feed bowl, then go over and knock the bowl so that a large portion of chop and pony nuts fell out. Spot would then proceed to eat the spilled contents with a look that said, 'Oh sorry, might as well finish that off seeing as it's spilt.' Misty's look was more of 'For God's sake!' but he never stopped Spot from eating. Misty's patience never ceased to amaze me.

It was midsummer again. Daylight can last as late as 11 o'clock at night in this part of the world. I sat with my horses in the field, just watching their blurred white outlines, being in the moment that belongs to horses, which doesn't care if it is 11 o'clock or any other artificially imposed human time, but is rather guided by the sun or the moon and the stars in the sky. I'd watched them though all the seasons now, several times over, seen herd dynamics develop and change until all the members settled down into an accepted, easy compromise.

Sitting with them that warm summer night, with the evening scent of the grass and the warm unmistakable smell of horses in the air, I came to realise just how lucky I was. Not lucky in the sense that the police officer had used after the assault, as in lucky not to have been killed; not lucky in inhabiting a comfortable, socially connected world and not lucky in having had an easy life behind me and the expectation of one in the future. Now I knew what luck or good fortune was: to be alive and enjoying this priceless moment, this day, every day. With the horses, I had found a comfortable place, felt able to accept and be accepted in that liminal world between the closed-off and excluding autistic world and the frightening, inaccessible outer world. They had become the family I never felt I had, and if it hadn't been for the assault, none of this might have happened.

Sitting there on that night, it occurred to me that probably once you start looking closely there are very many people in the world who are cut off or have limited options, people who might like to experience some of this magic I now had with the horses every day.

Spot and Alfie in particular were a magnet for people who were drawn towards their cute spotty appearance, amazed by their small size, intrigued by their lovely, trusting, friendly natures. Sometimes I would turn up at the field, which was overlooked by a public park, and find what amounted to a queue of people waiting in turn to pat them over the wall whilst the two spotties milked the occasion for all they were worth, loving the attention, the adulation, the carrots. Their effect seemed to cut across everyone: it seemed that hardly anybody could pass the field without wanting to talk to them. And this was in a rural area where people probably saw horses in fields every day. Moreover, these were people who were mobile, who could go out and see them pretty much whenever they wanted to.

Perhaps it was memories of my own unfulfilled dreams of being around horses as a child that got me thinking; perhaps it was also memories of that amazing transformation Minder had worked all those years ago, when just by going into a room he had had a seemingly miraculous effect on people. Anyway, it seemed to me that more people should be able to enjoy this, to have access to it if they wanted. Of course, it wouldn't suit everybody but, going on the response Alfie and Spot got every day of the week, the chances were that it would appeal to most people and moreover that Alfie and Spot would enjoy it. It seemed that, no matter how many people crowded round them, they enjoyed the attention and, more importantly, they were well behaved and polite and gentle.

I thought it was time for Spot and Alfie to start a new career.

20

a pony in the bedroom

I had left the Probation Service, having stuck it out for significantly longer than any other job I had ever done. Being there had been draining, but it had kept my social skills going and I had built up a tolerance (if never much of a liking) for having to be around others. Working, I had to admit, did keep me at least marginally socially connected and it probably saved me from the risks of solipsism, with its pitfalls of self-absorption, but I was never able to wholly commit myself when I was there – my *self* went on somewhere else, and I counted the minutes on the wall clock until I could be reunited with it and the horses and the dogs.

Handing in my notice was a great feeling – it lasted till the next day when I realised there were still going to be bills to pay. I was trying to make ends meet for me and four ponies on the proceeds of some properties I had bought, but looking at the balance sheets it was obvious that this arrangement could not go on indefinitely. I needed to earn some more money, if only a bit. After a period of unemployment, I opted for the job I thought would be easiest to get into and applied for a part-time post in a care home. There is a reason why there are so many care home jobs available, even in times of recession: in care work the pay is appalling, the responsibilities immense and status and appreciation practically non-existent. This is true in a good nursing home. How it works in a bad one, I have no idea.

I worked in a good one. Standards were high; residents were treated well and with respect. This was not always the case for the staff, especially newcomers like me, expecting that a job offering minimum wage was not going to be too demanding. Some of the staff were pleasant; most remained in exclusive cliques where outsiders were not particularly welcome.

I made a serious faux pas on my first day by sitting at the wrong table during the break in the staff room. It was empty and next to the television. Never having watched daytime TV, I was intrigued by what was happening on the programme blasting out and, as always, when something interests me I blocked out everything else and became mono-focussed. I watched in appalled fascination as the nation sought to wash its dirty laundry in the public washing machine that is reality television. When it was time to go back to work, I sensed something was wrong. There were other people sitting next to me, silently glaring at me.

'That's where the cleaners sit,' I was told later by a nice young senior carer who was showing me the ropes. '*Always.*' I never sat there again.

I didn't know much about dementia. Despite the efforts of various charities, it still seems to remain largely hidden away. In the home I saw where it was hiding. Suddenly I was engaging with a 93-year-old lady who told me she was waiting for her mother to pick her up from school. Another lady who had lived at the home for ten years asked every night if it was time to go home. She could never find her room unassisted. Others lived in a frightening, paranoid world where the carers and relatives were endlessly conspiring against them to get rid of them, take their money, sell their houses, which in many cases had been sold years before to pay for their care.

For others, the body had let them down. Infirmity, falls, sensory impairment and inability to perform basic routine tasks had left them helpless, dependent on others. Many felt degraded, of little value, a burden and useless. A few went the other way and decided to milk the care system for all it was worth, endlessly pressing their buzzers for trivial requests, which was infuriating for the overworked staff.

It was a whole new world to me and it was also one where I was expected to know my place. I was supposed to perform routine tasks without question, and finding out about patients' backgrounds from their care plans was not encouraged amongst the lower orders to which I clearly belonged. No matter, because I enjoyed listening to residents and I have always got on better with older people. Many residents had photos and other memorabilia in their rooms, so it was easy to strike up a conversation about the past. Most people loved to talk – it helped give them back their sense of identity, it took them to a better place – and the more I talked to people, the more I found out about them, and the easier they were to work with. Another thing I discovered, to my surprise, was that even when dementia is quite advanced, many people seem to retain a sense of humour, able to see funny things in the present, if nowhere else. Age seemed to let down barriers – people who had grown up in straight-laced societies, many of them still hung over from the Victorian era, seemed to find in old age that it didn't really matter if you told a smutty joke or made a scatological reference. There were no longer parents around to shock or children to protect and set an example to. I spent a lot of time laughing when I was with residents.

Social history, especially of the twentieth century, fascinated me. In the absence of a personal time scale/continuum or sense of connectedness, history has always provided me with a context and pointers. I could rarely make any meaningful connections between the past, present and future in my own life, but I could understand and piece together the grand trajectory sweep of human progress and regress that is history. My own formal A-level history education had gone up to 1914 and had been relentlessly political, but now I found myself talking to people about what they did on the day the First World War ended, how tractors took over from shire horses on the farms, getting the first ever telephone in the village, surviving on handouts in the hungry 1930s… The Second World War figured prominently in most people's memories: I met former Land Girls, Bevin Boys, and even a member of the Dambuster crew. Ex-RAF pilots told me about their sense of detachment when bombing German cities ('We had to defeat the Huns, you see, they were the enemy'), I learned about the best ways to pass time in an air-raid shelter, how to cook with powdered eggs, and how the only thing not rationed during the war was sex ('It was the best time we ever had'). Memories of the day before or what had happened in the morning might be sketchy to non-existent to totally fabricated, but stories of the past were vivid.

Lots of people had grown up around working horses which had names like Bonny and Blossom and Dobbin. It seemed there was no area of life that hadn't relied on horsepower up until the earlier twentieth century and beyond, from the ice-cream cart, the furniture removers, doctors gigs, laundry, coster vans, butchers, bakers, candlestick makers… Some people remembered parents and grandparents driving carts for a living or working directly with horses on the farms, or the arrival of the 'black brigade' (horse-drawn hearses pulled by black horses); others had fond memories of feeding working horses apples by the roadside or running out with a shovel when a cart went past in the hope of getting some manure for the vegetable patch; one lady of over 100 who had been a farmer's wife told me how she had bottle-fed an orphaned foal which thought itself part of the human herd ever after and was happy to walk into her kitchen if she would let it. Other less savoury memories were of seeing horses beaten to pull heavy loads up a hill or killed down in the mines. The stories were endless and my time was limited. Even in the best nursing homes, it seems that the thing so much wanted by residents – to spend time talking and being with someone – is the thing in shortest supply. Days in care homes can be long and boring. I wanted to do something to liven it up.

For those who had limited family contact – in fact, the majority of residents at the home – the staff became substitute family. True to my autistic nature, I was happy to engage with residents as long as I could return to my own private, shut-off world after work. I was also happy to share a select amount of information about myself and began to tell residents about the horses (actually, horses were the one topic of conversation I could carry on all day). Residents who could converse always asked me about the ponies: they followed the exploits of Alfie and Spot with interest and often remembered surprisingly well what they had been up to or what I was planning to do with them. I showed them photos and so often heard people say, 'I really wish I could see them,' that I began to ask myself that most productive of questions: 'Why not?'

One day, a lady called Kathleen was telling me how as a child she had never had any pets of her own but would constantly rescue stray cats or injured hedgehogs or birds, bringing them home and keeping them in the garden shed, much to her parents' wrath. Kathleen was diabetic, nearly blind and she had no one. She spent her days by the window in her room, listening to the birds. I told her about the ponies. 'I'd love to meet them,' she said. 'It would really make my day.'

I decided I was going to try to make Kathleen's day.

On the surface of it, there are quite a few reasons why one shouldn't take ponies into care homes. Just a few include:

Ponies are not domestic animals in the sense that dogs and cats are – an indoor environment is alien to them.

Ponies cannot be confined to a cage.

Ponies cannot be house-trained.

Ponies are flight animals which can spook and bolt easily.

Ponies (even small ones) are bigger than the biggest dog.

Ponies can kick, bite, tread on toes, swing round and bump into people.

Ponies are not predictable animals and can be frightened by sudden moves, strange noises and strange smells.

In spite of all that, I still thought it was an idea worth trying. I knew from my experience of being around the spotty ponies that they somehow weren't like 'normal' equines and seemed in many ways to be closer to dogs than horses. Very little seemed to faze them – they were brave, curious and infinitely sociable.

Alfie and Spot had been very well handled – you could touch any part of them, approach them from behind without warning and stroke them, take food from their food buckets whilst they were eating, crawl under their bellies if you so desired. And they knew what their boundaries were in the human field; they knew that kicking, biting or any form of rude behaviour was considered totally unacceptable and would be dealt with accordingly, and as a result they never demonstrated any. Perhaps more importantly, they had been treated as horses, not play things; they had been given respect and were expected to give it back. They were confident in me as a leader and that they were loved and looked after and treated fairly, and because they knew their place in the herd, they were willing to follow my lead. They had been exposed to many different situations from an early age and accepted large crowds pressing around them and making a fuss of them as natural. So far so good.

But how would they cope with going inside, being around frail, elderly and sometimes eccentric people? How would they cope with Zimmer frames and wheelchairs, the sounds of televisions and alarms going off? There was only one way to find out.

I broke out of my usual reticence and approached the care-home owner where I worked and suggested bringing a pony on a visit. He was enthusiastic and told me about the benefits previous animals had brought – spring lambs brought by a worker who had hand-reared them, chickens and, of course, the brilliant PAT (Pets As Therapy) dogs.

A pony visit was something new. It would entail a risk assessment, although, as the manager said, the potential benefits of animals tended to outweigh potential risks by a long way. I composed a risk assessment which looked at potential areas of damage. The main issues were: kicking, biting, treading on toes, knocking people over, pooing on carpet, peeing on carpet, damage to furniture, bolting horse, rearing horse, bucking horse, biting horse...

It was quite a formidable list really.

'Doesn't seem to be anything too major,' the boss said when I showed it to him, and, with the help of the activity coordinators who were very enthusiastic about it, a date was duly booked.

The visit nearly didn't happen. Objections started to be raised as soon as word got out that a pony was coming to visit the home.

'There's no way a pony's going to be coming on my ward,' I was told by one of the nurses.

'You can't bring a pony in here.' This from a senior carer.

I accepted that we would probably have to remain outside (in fact, I was rather hoping we would at that stage), but the negativity and dinosaur stance of 'It's never happened before so we can't do it' and 'You don't bring ponies into places like this' rankled slightly. For residents with limited futures and only the prospect of more pain and more deterioration in their condition, anything that makes the day seem better, even if it is only a short-term, momentary distraction, is surely a bonus.

Memories of reactions to Minder and of my own experience of healing through animals bolstered my determination. I knew it would be a good thing if Alfie (I'd decided to take him as the older pony) could cope. Everything about Alfie suggested to me that he would. He was, as I have mentioned, the quietest, most gentle pony I have ever met. If any pony could do it, he could. Anyway, I had backing from on high, so the visit was going to happen.

Alfie was washed and brushed to within an inch of his spots coming off. It was a hot summer day when I pulled up at the home with the horsebox and Alfie inside. I was glad of the weather: it meant we could stay outside (which also meant I wouldn't have to worry too much about the possibility of anything coming out of his back end – although on most journeys the motion of the engine tended to ensure that it was over and done with in the horsebox before we arrived).

I unloaded Alfie and tied him up for a last brush. Within minutes, a crowd had gathered, mainly of workers who had come down from the wards to look at him. Others leaned out of windows from above. Word was going out: 'There's a pony outside!'

Everyone was smiling and a barrage of comments and questions arose.

'That is so gorgeous!'

'Is he yours?'

'What's he called? How old is he?'

'Is that a Shetland? Is that a horse or a pony? Where do you keep him? How big will he grow?'

'I thought I was dreaming when I saw him.'

The questions rained down. I have since answered them many, many times, but on this occasion it brought home to me just how much interest a small pony in an unusual context can arouse – and this amongst people who were working and were not confined to the four walls of their room or the limited horizons of a care home or hospital. In the scheme of things, a pony is small, but when horizons are limited, it can make a vast difference.

And then it was time to meet the residents who had been brought down to an enclosed courtyard area for the visit. I walked Alfie into the centre of a group of about 30 people, many sitting in wheelchairs. As he walked in, the sound that I would later come to know so well arose: a collective 'Aww, look at that' rippled round the room as more and more people noticed him. I decided the best thing to do was take him round to meet people individually, so that anyone who wanted to pat him would have the opportunity. A more physically able lady, who nonetheless had quite severe dementia, walked up to him. She was often a difficult lady, understandably infuriated that her efforts to communicate proved futile, that no one seemed to help her when she asked where she could get the bus to school or tell her what time her mother was coming that day. On this occasion with Alfie, she wasn't cross – she was smiling as I had never seen her smile before. She began to stroke him and, when I handed her a brush, made a wonderful job of his mane. I was starting to get a good feel about it all.

I led Alfie around. He had never seen a wheelchair before but he took it very calmly in his stride (just a few weeks prior to writing this I witnessed how two fairly relaxed ponies took fright at the sight of one when a disabled rider came into a riding arena in a wheelchair – it reminded me of just how much I take for granted with the spotties). In fact, for people sitting down, Alfie was just the right height to be patted, stroked, brushed and admired. For those who were a little nervous (surprisingly few), he was happy just to stand still and be looked at. One lady who I had known on the ward burst into song: 'What's it all about Alfie?' The same lady rarely spoke otherwise.

Talking to people individually, letting them look at and pat Alfie if they wanted, answering questions and telling them about him seemed to be a vital part of the benefit of bringing him. With Alfie (and any other animal probably), there was an immediate icebreaker, a topic of conversation in the present moment, which for some people was the only world that existed. As I later went on to do more and more visits, I found out as well that the pony was often only the opening gambit, allowing people to chat about themselves, to give them time to talk.

To round off the visit, we were asked to go into the lounge of one of the wards. I really had no idea how Alfie would react to this, how sights and sounds, the feel of carpet or laminate flooring under his feet, maybe the blast of a television, the clinking of cutlery, different smells – all of these things that are not part of a horse's natural environment – would seem to him. But Alfie followed me in obediently and didn't bat an eyelid. When he entered the large lounge area, again a loud collective 'Aww' rippled round the room. He seemed to transform the whole atmosphere just by being there. A lady of over 100 clicked at him to come over. Residents were wheeled in from other wards to meet him, including a lady locked into silence and immobility by a terrible stroke, who had been active in the past at local agricultural shows. I will never forget the smile on her face as she patted him with the limited movement she had in one arm. Kathleen met him too. She put her arm around his neck. 'I'd've liked to have kept you in my shed too,' she said.

'Thank you so much for bringing him,' said one resident, a rather well-to-do lady whose mother, she told me, used to hunt side-saddle in the Edwardian era. 'It's brought back so many happy memories.'

Of the 60 or more people – staff, residents and relatives – who saw Alfie that day, I don't think that one didn't smile. People talked about the visit for weeks after. Photos with Alfie appeared in a large number of residents' rooms. Little Alfie, who is a mere 36 inches at the withers, had been a big hit.

It was to be the start of many visits. As news about the ponies spread, along with local media attention, requests to see them increased. Soon my younger pony, Spot, was going too, happy to follow in Alfie's more confident footsteps until he knew what was required of him when he went into a crowded building; then he would happily go on his own, glad of the individual attention he received, with no Alfie to nose him out of the way. People began to volunteer to go with me, which meant we could take two ponies at a time. Volunteers from the local Riding for the Disabled Association provided brilliant human- and horse-handling skills on visits.

I never really struggled too much on a personal level taking the ponies out on visits. If there was one thing I could always guarantee, it was that I would never be the main focus of attention – there were two spotty ponies upstaging me every time. I could therefore walk into a room full of strangers and feel fairly safe. Conversation focussed on the ponies too; there were always many questions, people recounting their personal experiences, people wanting to take photos of them, people asking if they could take them home with them…

There was, however, another obstacle to overcome. As horses can't (to the best of my knowledge) be house-trained – the flight instinct, roughage diet and a trickle-feeding digestive system evolved over millions of years militate against it – we were constantly on the lookout during visits for the possibility of horse droppings being deposited on the nice clean carpets of the health-and-safety-driven care homes. We didn't want to add to the work of the already overburdened staff by creating another cleaning job.

Worrying about what would come out of the ponies' back ends during a visit was a distraction and tended to make us want to rush the visit, thinking that if we got away with it for an hour, it would be unwise to push our luck any further. The vagaries of the British weather meant that the residents could rarely meet the ponies outside, and whilst the places we visited were generally fine if anything untoward did happen – the benefits were so great compared with this possible drawback – if there was any way we could avoid it, we wanted to do so.

I thought long and hard about it, trawling the internet in search of possible solutions. The likeliest source of help seemed to be harness makers and suppliers. Working carriage horses on the streets are often obliged to wear bags under their tails to collect the dung and prevent it fouling the streets in predominantly tourist areas. But finding anything that would fit a miniature pony seemed like a long shot.

All I can say is thank God for Google. It seems there's nothing you can't eventually find on the internet if you try hard enough and nothing you can't buy with a PayPal account at the press of a button. Somewhere in the northwest of America – Idaho, to be precise – a lady was making bags for catching the droppings of miniature horses.

'Are they for therapy ponies?' she asked when I rang up.

'Yes.' I was surprised. She had said 'therapy ponies' as if it were a natural thing, whereas, as far as I was aware, using ponies in this way was highly unusual if not totally unique. We chatted some more and I learned that, whilst by no means widespread, the use of ponies, or more usually the tiny American Miniature Horses, for indoor therapy in America was fairly accepted in some states. I also learned for the first time about Guide Horses, miniature horses and ponies used to do the work more usually done by guide dogs for blind people who, for cultural or health or other reasons, are unable to use dogs. Horses never cease to amaze me in what they can do for humans. Probably the best known example is Riding for the Disabled, but there are many other ventures now which look at equines as a source of healing and growth and learning.

The bags for the horses duly arrived. We have used them ever since with impressive results. Many care homes, day centres and special schools across the region owe a debt of gratitude to that lady in Idaho.

One thing I always wanted was for the ponies to be able to visit those unable or unwilling to get to communal areas downstairs. Kathleen, who had been my main inspiration for taking Alfie on his initial visit, was a case in point. For someone confined to the limits of one room, with no prospect of ever going anywhere, life can be slow and boring, and people are much more likely to become depressed. An animal that can go into someone's room can be a major source of pleasure, often providing a talking point for weeks after the visit. It is often also an incentive for family members to visit, especially children who might find the care home environment alien or intimidating but who would be queuing up to come if they knew there was a pony at the end of it. A pony visit could therefore turn into a family affair, or at the very least could ensure that a cut-off resident got some one-to-one time.

But there was another obstacle: stairs. The ponies were not keen on indoor steps and I was unwilling to work on persuading them to go up in the event that they might panic halfway and not have room to turn round. I also didn't want the ponies to do anything they were clearly unhappy about, but I was prepared to work with them on doing things that were simply new by giving them time to get used to whatever it was and rewarding them in stages when they had done it.

The problem was resolved for me one day on a visit to a care home. The activities organiser, Judith, whom I knew and who is also a horsewoman, said on our arrival, 'A lady upstairs really wants to see them. Can we take them up to her bedroom? It's on the first floor.'

I looked at Alfie and then at Spot who was being led behind in the corridor, his small hooves clipping on the laminate floor.

'Err, how?'

'They'll be all right in the lift, won't they?' Judith said.

There was only one way to find out.

Spot follows me anywhere given half a chance. I looked at the open lift. It was big enough to accommodate both of us, big enough for Spot to turn round – we could both walk straight back out if Spot was unhappy.

'Let's go,' I said to him. Spot walked into the lift quite happily. He did a double take at the mirror that faced him as he walked in and nickered softly to the handsome little spotty pony who was staring at him. I had a handful of Trebor mints ready to distract him as I pressed the lift button and the lift gave a small jolt as it moved upwards. Spot took the Trebor mint but continued to focus on his reflection. I held my breath as the lift moved from ground to first floor; it seemed to take forever. I doubt that Spot even noticed after the initial jolt. When we reached the first floor, he turned himself round and walked calmly out, stepping over the gap between the lift and the corridor as though it was the most natural thing in the world. Outside the lift a host of people were taking his photo and the exclamations were ringing:

'*I've got to show this to the kids!*'

'*I just don't believe that – it was amazing!*'

'*How long did it take you to train him to do that?*'

'*What a brilliant little pony!*'

Spot posed for them, lifting his head as if to say, *Yes, I'm pretty clever, aren't I?*

Alfie followed, slightly more anxiously, mainly, I felt, because he was uncertain whether he could squeeze himself round in such a tight space as he was a bit fatter than Spot.

The little ponies had done it.

So the ponies made their first visit to the bedroom of a lovely lady called Maureen who had not been outside of it for many months. The ponies' heads were just the right height to fit over the bed rail. They were surprisingly adept at manoeuvring around pieces of furniture, and they did not mind the crush of people around them. They did it as if they had been doing it all their lives.

Since then they have been in many strange places, including care homes, hospices, churches, special schools, community centres, hotels, pubs, shops... They have posed for television and stood stock-still at motorbike rallies. None of this is in itself important, but what does matter is the mini miracle they work with people again and again. So often they have drawn people out who were stuck in difficult or cut-off worlds, bringing out words, smiles, touch. I've seen selectively mute autistic children break out of their silent worlds to talk and reach out to them, watched as people at the end of life make a gesture or smile in their direction, seen how severely depressed people burst into laughter.

None of it surprises me.

afterword
horses as healers

I've read many claims about the mystical healing power of horses: that they are our earthly spiritual teachers, embodiments of female intuitive power, archetypes from the subconscious, mediators between earthly and psychic realms... My own view is rather more pragmatic and I can only (in true autistic style) speak of what I have personally experienced and witnessed. For me, horses have been the mediators between my inner and outer worlds, not in a mystical sense but in the sense of providing a safe middle ground between the two, a place where I can stand and draw on both parts, which brings a wholeness of its own. Being with horses is the place between being isolated and cut off and overwhelmed and anxious.

When our lives are broken and damaged, or when reaching across the divide, as in the case of autism, is too risky or too frightening or simply not something you want to do, animals can step in, providing the middle ground of contact with a sentient being which is accepting, loyal and not judgemental. Animals provide those of us who respond to them (which is not everybody) with a neutral presence, free of the ambivalence we may bring to human encounters. When that ambivalence is shot through with fear, when trust has been destroyed, when every human encounter is a potential source of pain or a reminder of one's difference, the neutral presence can be like a homecoming, the chance to breathe deeply and freely again in the presence of another, to know that you are not entirely alone and that you will not be overwhelmed, judged or destroyed.

As an adult, I came to horses by chance as a way of coping with post-traumatic stress. Post-traumatic stress had brought me up against the limitations of learning and logic, those so-called higher human faculties which we think place us above the animal kingdom and which I had so often fallen back on in the absence of a social or emotional understanding. In a real-life threatening situation, my rational thinking brain had failed to protect me; it was essentially useless – I was brought down from the cerebral realms to a world in which I was disembodied and disassociated and no amount of thinking was going to help. Animals, that great antidote to the cerebral, were to prove more beneficial than anything else in helping me deal with the trauma. The presence of dogs who shared my space night and day was to be crucial in grounding me, bringing me back to earth, however fleetingly, when I had drifted out too far into the traumatised world.

In the early days of riding horses at the riding school, when I was still living in a frozen space due to the assault, I had abdicated my physical self, abandoning it as a place that I felt was no longer safe. Horses played a crucial part in getting me 'back inside myself' by teaching me to reconnect and focus on my body in a way that I was willing to do. In riding, I reclaimed that connection; I learned to live inside myself again.

Through riding, I also discovered that by being around horses I had found a place I could feel safe again amongst a species that, understanding implicitly what it is to live in the world as a potential victim/prey, allowed me in to share its world – to feel that I was not alone in a threatening universe. By sitting on a horse, I was allowed into the horse's space and allowed another into my space; I shared that most relaxing of movements, the four-beat time of a walking horse, an action that is known for releasing the feel-good hormone oxytocin. I was with another and it felt good.

Horses brought many gifts to help deal with post-traumatic stress: they taught me to take control again, to trust, to go outside of my own house willingly and thereby overcome the phobias that were keeping me locked inside. They taught me to focus in the present and to let go of the past; they showed me how to breathe deeply and relax.

This in itself was an amazing piece of good fortune. That horses went on to provide a journey of discovery, which would lead to an alternative place to my closed-off autistic world and thereby transform it, goes beyond good fortune. As someone with an autistic spectrum condition, I still remain unusually isolated, cut off by my lack of urge to deal with the social world to any great degree. This is not an inevitable consequence for people with autism; it is simply the choice I have made, and it is an informed choice which may also change in time.

Whereas interactions with humans are complex, usually verbal, sometimes confusing, invariably stressful and bring with them a whole raft of potential sensory overload, animals generally and horses in particular have a quality of stillness about them, a simplicity which is restful to be around. There is none of the invasive white noise of human small talk, the complex display of emotions of humans which requires a response – but which response? To go from daily human encounters requiring a highly developed arsenal of interpretive skills to simply spending time with horses in the field every day can offer much-needed respite in the autistic world with its daily and lifelong struggle to function in the social world.

In terms of managing to cope with the world, animals have made a phenomenal difference. That particular time zone that belongs to horses, grazing animals governed by the natural cycles, grounds me, brings me naturally out of my closed-off world, back to the earth, to the seasons, to the diurnal and annual changes. Horses teach me to stay on the earth, to be in the present moment, to deal with the concrete reality in front of me.

And there are crossover effects from being around animals that have implications for how people with autism may be able to relate better to humans. I had found with my first dog, Minder, that he paradoxically brought out human characteristics in me which were largely frozen or hidden – the capacity to reach out, talk willingly rather than from necessity, the attachment that lasts beyond the immediate presence, the ability to nurture and to care. This was not something I actively sought but it was a by-product of that and other animal relationships, something I learned and participated in willingly and naturally with none of the usual stress or ambivalence or fear. Being around animals has in its way taught me a lot about how to be around people at a social level.

I know now that to be in and part of a herd is not to always be lost or overwhelmed but can sometimes allow you to be more yourself, to breathe deeply and relax, and know that someone else will share the burden of protection in an uncertain world.

And I lose nothing by it. Whereas in the human world I have so often felt threatened, diminished, forced to retreat and disappear, in the horse world I can maintain my wholeness, power, identity and dignity in the presence of other sentient beings. With horses, my constant struggle to feel linked to a time and place, a *here* and *now*, something perhaps denied me through the disconnectedness of autism, was resolved. I could be in a *here* and *now* with them and I could feel wholly at peace. These are benefits that over time I have noticed myself being able to transfer into the human social world, having had the chance to experience and practise them on a daily basis in the neutral, accepting environment of animals.

In my world, horses are a gift, a blessing that is not limited but which overflows. It was therefore a gift which ultimately I felt able to share with others, to bring the therapeutic benefits that I had experienced to anyone else who wanted it. In the autistic world, the world of the enclosed and cut-off self, being able to reach out spontaneously to the world is a massive act. It is an enormous tribute to the overflowing gifts that horses bring that I was able to and felt moved to pass it on.